In memory of my father, my brother, and my in-laws. Pray for the elderly, those struggling with dementia/Alzheimer's and other terminal illnesses. Bless all caregivers for their service.

ACKNOWLEDGMENTS

I am forever grateful to all the people who were willing to get involved and helped in my caregiving efforts. Special thanks go to the DHR social worker, the Alzheimer's Association, doctors and lawyers, neighbors who assisted in many different ways, friends and co-workers who lent a sympathetic ear, my mother and husband who provided emotional support and caregiving, church programs, church people, and Hospice.

A big hug goes to my cousin, Marilyn, for her editing of this book. She was able to read my mind and heart perfectly and help me better describe my experiences over these years. I am forever indebted for her willingness to provide her expertise in this undertaking.

Thank you all for helping me come to grips with the terrible reality of Alzheimer's disease and making it to the other side - maybe not unscathed, but more knowledgeable, appreciative of life and accepting of circumstances.

DEDICATION

This book is dedicated to my mother. Her example of love and caring has been a continual inspiration to me.

PREFACE

I had heard the terms dementia and Alzheimer's before, but little did I know about the realities of the disease, the specific ways it would affect me and my beloved family members or how many years the nightmare of this tragedy would continue.

I knew that people often lost their memory and got confused, usually when they grew older, but I believed I would be there to help my family remember and guide them through activities they could no longer do unassisted. How uneducated and naïve I was!

As we age, we may experience moments of forgetfulness, but that forgotten memory usually returns to us quickly. For a person with dementia, the brain circuits become broken. The brain is shrinking and dying and it gradually robs the person of memories on a permanent basis and prevents them from performing previous normal activities and the ability to be self-sufficient. They become totally dependent on others for their well being and care. With Alzheimer's, a degenerative brain disease, plaques and tangles (resulting from amyloid and tau proteins) have been found which kill cells in the brain, totally debilitating the patient over time.

Years ago people who most likely had dementia were labeled crazy or senile. In 1906, Alois Alzheimer documented dramatic shrinkage and abnormal deposits he noticed in a patients' brain. It brought about a major change in thought from accepting more than normal memory loss as a part of old age, to the possibility of it being a disease that could be studied and potentially treated. Alzheimer's disease was officially named in 1910, but it was not until the 1980's when the Alzheimer's

Association was founded and great strides in research were made. In the 1990's, the first drugs to treat the symptoms were finally approved.

As I began my care journey I sought out others dealing with the disease. I knew of six people involved with parents' dementia. One friend had full time caregivers providing care to the mother in the mother's home. The second friend lasted a month providing care to her father before placing him in a care facility. The third friend's father-in-law was in a facility. Unhappy with their care and the long commute to visit him, he was moved into their house where she assumed care. After a year he was placed in a different facility. Also dissatisfied with their care, she hired a live-in caregiver to help out in her own home. The fourth friend's mother was in a SCALF (Specialty Care Assisted Living Facility – for those with memory issues) the whole length of her disease. The fifth friend moved her mother into her home after the mother drove off in her car and was missing for two days. She eventually placed her mother in a nursing home. A sixth acquaintance placed her mother in a facility once bathroom issues became too overwhelming. <u>None of these families provided full care themselves for the entire length of their parents' disease</u>.

My maternal grandfather may have had the onset of dementia, but in 1985, when he passed away, research was really just getting underway. During his last year of life I noticed a mental decline. He kept repeating the same jokes, as if they had never been told before. He battled cancer and wound up collapsing in his garden at the age of 84 from a heart attack. At that time I did not have first-hand experience in dealing with elderly mental issues or the need to provide full care.

My husband told me his grandmother had dementia. His parents placed her in a nursing home quickly, afraid she might forget to turn off the stove and burn the house down. She died a few months after entering the facility.

Twenty years later, around the year 2001, both of my husbands' parents began exhibiting memory issues and were eventually diagnosed with dementia/NOS (non-specific) and dementia/Alzheimer's. Around 2006 my own father was also stricken with the disease. It was obvious **all three** parents needed help desperately and I was determined to assist them the best I could.

The situation was relatively uncommon since both in-laws were incapacitated at the same time. Most people have only one parent going through the disease with the remaining parent able to provide some degree of spousal care. To complicate matters, my in-laws suffered abuse by another family member. My husband and I had to secure legal help, during which time his parents' conditions rapidly worsened.

Typically, available books and brochures focused on the stages of dementia. What my husband and I really needed was detailed information about exact things we might expect during the day-to-day experience of caring for our family members. Mostly we learned by trial and error and through members of the local Alzheimer's Association.

After particularly difficult days I documented what had happened and wrote down my feelings, mostly as therapy for myself. As time went on, I provided the information I had gathered to friends and co-workers to help educate them on the disease. Several of these people encouraged me to "write a book", which is how the idea for this effort began. As painful as it initially was to relive these experiences, it was an important step in my own grieving and recovery. Also, it might be a help to others in our same situation.

I am neither doctor, nor nurse, but I spent six years providing full care to my in-laws and to my father with dementia/Alzheimer's. I found each phase of this disease to be difficult and challenging. Luckily I was blessed with support from my husband, my mother, neighbors, friends, co-workers, family from afar, doctors, lawyers, community organizations, church and my God.

The following is the story of my personal journey as a caregiver detailing my sorrows and my joys, my successes and my failures.

Introduction to Me and My Family

Symptoms of dementia for my in-laws, Olivia and Jeremy, began when they were just 73 years old. My mother-in-law's dementia lasted for 15 years and my father-in-law's spanned approximately 11 years.

My own father started exhibiting memory issues at age 87. He lived another 8-1/2 years with Alzheimer's. My mother was 79 at the onset of Dad's disease. Mom had survived cancer, unlike my brother who battled it for six years before succumbing at the age of 45, his life cut so short. Mom now had severe osteoarthritis, diabetes and stage 3 kidney disease. I was working full-time and 47 years old. My husband Stan was self-employed, working full-time and 54.

A period of almost six years passed from our first awareness of my in-laws' mental symptoms until they required round-the-clock care. Two years later, Stan and I became their full time guardians. I was then 55 and Stan had just turned 62. Usually people of that age start to think about retiring. Life didn't turn out as we expected. I had always envisioned Stan and I having a retirement filled with travel and hobbies, but God seemed to have a different plan and calling for us. I don't regret the years we spent helping our parents. I wouldn't have given it up for anything.

All four of our parents, my husband and I went through a myriad of emotions during those years: denial, frustration, anger, resentment, grief, and finally acceptance. There were also many moments of joy, bonding and laughter that I will never forget.

You may find some of the suggestions included to be similar to the care of any elderly person, but many are specific to the care of a dementia patient. While every person's symptoms and behaviors are unique, and family dynamics and resources are different, I hope you find some help from this handbook, if only to know you are not alone.

I wish you luck and love in your journey.

TABLE OF CONTENTS

THE IN-LAWS 1

First Signs of Something Wrong 3
Inability to Perform Routine Tasks - General Confusion 5
Assistance in the Home and Banking 6
Wills and Durable Power of Attorney 6
I Seek and Gather Information 8
Initial Care Plan 8
The Denial Stage, Suspicion and Alienation 9
The Search for and Cost of Care Facilities 10
Misappropriation of Funds/Inability to Make Decisions 12
Decline in Their Condition 13
Safety Concerns 13
Help Rejected 14
Contacting the Local Dept. of Human Resources (DHR) 15
A Safe Haven 16
The Police and Restraining Order 17
Where Do We Go From Here? / Hospice 18
Review of Medications and Recent Medical History 18
Legal Drama-Search and Discovery of Assets 21
Loss of Memory and Falling 25
Some Health Improvement 27
Care Aids 28
Hallucinations and Psychosis 28
Daily Life 29
Search for In-Home Caregivers 31
Support Options 32
Combative Behavior 33
Lack of Available Care Facilities 34
Mother-in-Laws Letters 34
Father-in-Law's Final Days 38
Short Term Memory Loss 40
A New Home 41

A Short Break for Us 42
We Move Again 42
Mental Effect of the Incapacitation Ruling 43
Day-to-Day Life 44
Breaking and Losing Things 51
Physical Improvement but Increase in Memory Loss 52
Short Excursions Outside of the Home 53
Issues with Eating 54
The Toll on Us 55
Time Off / Finding "Sitters" 59
Housebound 60
Loss of Vision, Hearing, Reading and Writing Skills 61
Interesting Dress 62
Decorations and Stuffed Toys 62
We Learn As We Go 63
Emotional Support 63
Hoarding 64
Laundry, Clothes and Dressing Issues 64
Things in Disarray / The Messy Phase 65
The Naked Phase 66
Long Term Memory Loss 67
Further Decline and Congestive Heart Failure 67
Advanced Mobility Issues 68
Going "Home" 71
Another Hospital Stay and Medicare Home Health 72
Difficulty Sitting and Standing/Needing Proper Furniture 73
Incontinence and Contamination in the House 74
Belligerent 76
Working From Home 78
Baby Proofing 78
On the Wait List 78
We Go Away 79
Sudden Cessation of Walking and Eating 81
The End 81

MY FAMILY 83

The Beginning of Health Issues 84
Loss of Memory and Abilities 85
Vacations 92
Medication is Started 93
How Can We Take Care of Them All? 93
Depression 93
Daily Life 94
He Escapes 96
Further Decline/He Doesn't Know Us 97
Somewhere in the Past 100
Isolation/In the Dark 103
How to Occupy His Time 103
Lost in the House 105
Loss of Senses 105
Scared and Clinging 106
Hallucinations 107
Increased Personal Care 108
Nudity Phase 109
Dad on the Wait List 110
Changing Medications and No Sleep 110
Loss of Communication but Still Praising God 111
Music Therapy 112
Stress and At Battle 113
Search for Care Facility Openings 115
Bathroom Issues 116
Safety Concerns and Out of Control Behavior 116
Babbling and Unable to Feed Self – Full Care Status 118
Geriatric Psychiatric Hospital 119
End of Life Care Decision 123
To Die at Home 125
The Last Two Weeks 128
He Leaves Us 131

CONCLUSION 133

Words of Encouragement and Faith 138

APPENDIX 140

Timeline of Alzheimer's Discovery and Research 140
Caregiving Aids 142
Dementia Comment and Translation 151
Glossary 152
Reference 160

THE IN-LAWS

Stan and I had been married for 6 years. We had what I considered a good relationship with his parents and routinely went every Sunday to their house for a home-cooked meal. His mother, Olivia, was always a gracious hostess. We enjoyed times together, even taking several joint summer vacations to the beach. Stan's father, Jeremy, was typically quiet and didn't say much, but was pleasant.

Olivia had spent 25 years working for the civil service until she retired at the age of 55. It was now 18 years later. Jeremy had been in the Navy and then also worked for the civil service until his retirement.

One of Olivia's hobbies was sewing. She had made costumes for the local theater guild performances. She also sewed quilts and made a special one as a gift for our bed.

Olivia and Jeremy were active in their church and helped serve communion. Olivia was quite religious and had gone to a private Catholic school growing up.

Olivia and Jeremy went on two cruises and both of them loved fishing. They purchased a treadmill and were trying to keep physically fit.

Stan and I were fairly active in his parents' lives, at least as much as we could be while working full-time. We both helped his parents pick out new home furnishings. Olivia and I shared recipes and cooking ideas and I assisted her with home decorating. I also picked out a computer for my in-laws which I set up and provided instructions on.

There were other family members. Stan's sister lived out of state and had some issues. We rarely saw her. There were accusations about my father-in-law, behavioral problems and skeletons in the family closet that most people did not know about. While every family has problems, these issues were never resolved and they continued to fester through the years and cause frequent rifts between the family members. I often felt like I was caught in the middle. To any outsider, all was fine. Stan's father had also had an affair and left the family for a short time during the children's younger years. Stan's youngest brother had committed suicide at age 22. My husband and I did not get along with his remaining brother, Jason. Jason was lazy and a bully; always picking a fight with others including Stan or me when we were together.

In the past, Jason had beaten his younger brother, breaking bones in his face. He had threatened to beat up Stan. Recently, he started an altercation in a store and had to be escorted out. Jason was also threatening to beat up other acquaintances. He was bad news.

Jason seemed to manipulate his family, especially his mother. She bailed him out of several lawsuits involving sloppy work and unfinished jobs. She felt sorry for him, especially when he went through his third divorce. This ex-wife had a Restraining Order against him. My in-laws allowed Jason to live with them when he claimed he could not find work and had nowhere to go.

Due to our discord with Jason, Stan and I eventually told his parents that we would come to see them only if Jason was not present. Our visits never went well when he was around. Stan's mother said she just wished we could all get along. She avoided conflict at all cost. She was the type of person to sweep problems under the rug and pretend there was nothing amiss.

In my opinion, Jason was the ultimate con man who had perfected the art of sweet talking women into marriage. Then he would quit working and his wives were left to support and house him. Jason did this repeatedly throughout his life with many failed marriages and relationships.

He was totally banned from one church and that engagement cancelled. During another engagement, two sons of this fiancée showed up on my in-laws' doorstep. They said they were going to kill Jason for swindling their mother out of her home. My father-in-law told them not to kill Jason; "just break his legs, maybe he'll learn his lesson". Stan and I never learned if these two brothers continued to hunt Jason, or if they just left and returned to their homes, several states away.

First Signs of Something Wrong

Both parents had several "episodes" prior to their diagnosis of dementia. The first episode we knew of was when we accompanied Stan's parents to his fathers' Navy reunion. We drove in separate vehicles. On the way there, Jeremy rear-ended our car, so we began questioning his driving ability. The second morning on the trip, Olivia told Stan and me that Jeremy had become disoriented, didn't know who she was and was asking what she was doing in his hotel room. Olivia was quite upset. At the time, I thought my father-in-law probably had too much to drink while reminiscing with his old war buddies. I quickly put the issue out of my mind.

Shortly after the trip, Stan's mother reported that Jeremy had become confused again. He had trouble finding his way home from the food store, which was just across the street. He would often walk there to buy groceries.

Olivia also had several episodes prior to her dementia diagnosis. Stan and I planned another trip with his parents to the beach. We arrived to find that his mother had been taken to the hospital for a psychotic episode. She had watched a television special showing the events of 9/11. Olivia believed what she was seeing was happening right where she was. The hospital examined her, gave sedatives and sent her back to the condo for the remainder of the vacation.

Both parents seemed to be doing well until several months later, when Olivia was admitted to the hospital after claiming to have had a migraine headache for days. The staff at the hospital put a sign on her door requesting complete darkness and quiet. They told Stan and me that his mother had taken off all her clothes and had streaked down the hall.

After Olivia was released, I mentioned the incident to her. She was horrified because that behavior was so foreign to her normal modesty. However, she seemed to recover from the episode.

I believe that both parents, but especially Olivia's psychotic episodes and migraines, were likely signs of **_Stage 1 (mild dementia)_** with changes in the brain due to shrinkage and nerve cell death. **Symptoms were just now becoming noticeable to us, but the disease had probably started at least a year or two earlier**. *The early stage of dementia can last from two to four years. During this stage the short term memory starts to be affected. The person becomes* *disoriented, and has trouble planning, but can still manage personal care.*

Olivia had numerous risk factors which may have contributed to her dementia, including diabetes, high blood pressure, thyroid issues, and a treatable B12 deficiency. She had also had a TIA (transient ischemic attack, or mini-stroke caused by a clot) and required a stent in one carotid artery about two years before Stan and I got married. This may have caused insufficient blood flow to the brain.

Inability to Perform Routine Tasks - General Confusion

Within a year after the first signs of something wrong with both in-laws, I noticed that my mother-in-law was no longer able to perform routine household activities. She couldn't coordinate making meals, and was unable to complete simple tasks that she had always done before, such as cleaning house.

Olivia, who had always loved to sew, would talk about making another quilt, but never seemed to get started. She could make no headway on anything or follow through with plans.

Stage 2 (moderate dementia) symptoms were now in full swing. *In Stage 2, the person can no longer perform routine tasks, has lost short term memory and the ability to know day and time. The person will get lost or lose things, be confused by relationships, and need accompaniment everywhere. Finally, there is suspicion and hallucinations. This stage can last from <u>two to ten years</u>.*

Assistance in the Home and Banking

Olivia needed help cleaning the house, so I contacted a local agency and arranged for cleaning service to come every other week. Olivia was pleased with the first cleaning lady, but she didn't care for the others that followed and she cancelled the service.

During subsequent visits to their home, I noticed that my in-laws' bills were being returned because the checks were made out incorrectly or had been sent unsigned. Olivia said she trusted me and wanted help. She added me on their bank account to assist should there be a need or an emergency.

I also began running errands for my in-laws when they couldn't seem to manage getting out. Jeremy was increasingly unsteady on his feet and had fallen. I picked up a walker for him to use.

Wills and Durable Power of Attorney

Concerned about their future, Stan and I spoke to his parents about possible long term care. After reviewing information they received, everyone agreed that a lot of money could be wasted if long term care was never required.

Olivia and Jeremy sent a list of sentimental personal belongings to their three children with instructions that the children should select any items they wished to have after their parents' deaths. Other than these small keepsakes, there was no mention of how assets such as my in-laws' house or money was to be divided.

Stan and I inquired whether my in-laws' Wills were up to date. We discovered they were not. Stan's parents needed to select a new Executor since Olivia's brother, who was named in their Wills, had died a year earlier. Stan's parents promised to have their Wills updated.

My in-laws also had no Living Will or <u>Durable</u> Power of Attorney (POA) over their medical care and decisions should they no longer be capable of doing so themselves. They now appointed Stan with medical POA, but no discussions were made concerning other possible living alternatives should they be required. Stan and I did know that his parents had crypts at a local cemetery. Their funerals had been pre-paid, so at least that had been arranged.

A few months passed, but Olivia and Jeremy had not revised their Wills. Stan set up an appointment to take them to an Elder Care lawyer. On the day of the appointment, Olivia called Stan saying something had come up and they would have to reschedule the meeting.

In the weeks and months that followed, Olivia began telling Stan and me different stories whenever we saw her. At first we couldn't figure out why she was lying to us about everything. We couldn't decide if she was playing some game, or whether it was due to some other issue.

Stan and I didn't know it was dementia affecting his parents at that time. We just knew something was wrong and that they needed help. At this point, they were already too far along for them to take appropriate actions to help themselves.

I Seek and Gather Information

I asked my in-laws who their family doctor was and what prescriptions they were taking. I made laminated cards with the information to carry with me at all times and which Stan's parents carried on their person and in their vehicle.

I finally decided to call my in-laws' general practitioner to see if I could find out anything more about their health. The doctor volunteered that both of Stan's parents were suffering from ***dementia***. He said that each had less than half a functioning brain and that he had started Stan's mother on a low dose of Aricept. The Veterans Center was the primary care provider for Stan's father. The only way Stan's parents were functioning by themselves in their home was because they were working together. Even together, that equaled less than one full brain. I was free to call the doctor for updates.

Stan and I became worried that his parents would get lost in the neighborhood. I contacted the Alzheimer's Association and obtained "Safe Return" ID bracelets for them to wear. The bracelets listed "Memory Impaired" on the back and the phone number to the local Alzheimer's hot-line who would contact us if help was needed. I really don't know how often, if ever, Olivia and Jeremy actually wore the bracelets when they went out.

Initial Care Plan

It was now 2005, four years since the first signs of something wrong. As Stan and I were both working full-time, and Stan's brother Jason was still not working, he became the one, by default, to be in charge of his parents care. Stan and I lived a half hour away. While Stan and I were not totally comfortable with this plan, we assumed Jason would be responsible and help his parents.

The Denial Stage, Suspicion and Alienation

Even though Stan and I now knew his parents had dementia, both parents, but particularly Stan's mother, went into complete denial. Neither one would acknowledge or accept their diagnosis. This only made our attempts at helping them and getting proper treatment that much more difficult. Since Stan and I did not communicate well with his brother Jason, we were not informed about my in-laws on-going health issues. Their doctor, however, told me that both parents continued covering up their failings and were attempting to compensate for one another's decline.

Soon, Olivia began rejecting our help altogether and became alienated. In fact, she sent me a nasty note insisting I relinquish rights to their bank account. This I did, assuring her that I had never used the account for any purpose, had never had access to any of their checks, and had never reviewed or received any bank statements. I was really confounded and didn't know what I could possibly have done to cause my mother-in-law's change of heart. In addition, Olivia asked that Stan return the key to their house, which he did.

Looking back on these incidents, I'm sure that once Jason realized that I, not a blood relative, was on his parents' bank account, he was furious and insisted his parents remove me. I would have reacted the same way if the situation were reversed and involved my own parents. After all, I was just the daughter-"in-law". But at the time, I was very hurt by my mother-in-law's letter and I backed away from her.

Over the next six months, with Jason providing care to his parents, Stan and I saw them less. We weren't invited over often. At Easter, we just showed up at their house with a complete dinner and invited ourselves inside. Jason was not present at the time. The house, and especially the kitchen, was a wreck. There were dirty dishes piled high in the sink for what appeared to be days. Stan and I knew things were not right and that his parents really needed help, but we were unsure of what to do.

Stan had a practice of calling his parents daily to check up on them. There was a two day period when they couldn't be reached on the phone. On the third day Stan called their neighbor who told us that Olivia was in the hospital. We immediately went there and were told that Olivia had been admitted for severe diabetic issues, almost going into a coma.

We were also told by the nurse that Jason was now supposed to give Olivia insulin shots. Stan and I were very upset by this. We didn't trust Jason and he had obviously not been taking proper care of his mother. Stan and I believed some other form of care for his parents was necessary. We also did not know that Jason had somehow secured a new medical POA over his parents.

The Search for and Cost of Care Facilities

Stan and I started attending meetings of the local Alzheimer's Association to find out more about dementia and how others were handling it. The support group was a great tool for sharing and learning, but the meetings were only once a month. There were typically 8-10 people in attendance which didn't allow much time per person to speak in an hour. I tried to attend the luncheon meetings, but often my work deadlines prevented me from getting there. There was a night meeting at another location, but that meant me making another trip into town after dinner.

The Alzheimer's group leader provided her phone number if more one-on-one advice was needed. She recommended several local care facilities to look into. Over the next several months Stan and I began researching and visiting them believing this was where his parents needed to be. At first we looked at Assisted Living, but were told it sounded like his parents needed a Specialty Care Assisted Living Facility (SCALF) due to their memory issues. SCALF care meant Stan's parents would be in "lock down" where they could not go off the floor or wing by themselves and needed constant supervision. They would have many restrictions.

Our goal was to keep both of his parents together somewhere. We found that the typical cost in a SCALF was around $54,000 per person before incidentals (prescriptions, personal toiletry items and clothes). There were additional charges depending on how much other assistance was required.

If full care was needed, the costs averaged $92,000 or more per person per year. The two best facilities in town required $240,000 up front just for admission, and a high monthly rate.

Stan and I believed that my in-laws' annual income would be short in covering the cost for both of them in a SCALF. However, we thought they had several hundred thousand dollars in the bank, numerous money market accounts and CD's. With the sale of their home, there would be more than enough money to cover their future expenses.

Sadly, the patients at the SCALF's Stan and I visited seemed quite a bit worse than his parents. Most were slumped in a wheelchair, left alone and drooling.

We had not yet decided how best to approach Stan's parents about going to a SCALF, but we did find two which were acceptable to us. They were clean, had plenty of activities, the patients seemed well cared for and the homes had high ratings.

Misappropriation of Funds/Inability to Make Decisions

Several more months went by. Now, when Stan and I visited his parents, we noticed a lot of money being spent on new floors, new furniture, new appliances, and an expensive bed. Additionally, Olivia told us that Jason was **demanding money.** We responded by saying, "don't give him any or he will continue to demand it".

The treadmill and computer in their home had disappeared. Although both in-laws were incapable of using either item anymore, we were told that Jason had "taken them". Olivia then admitted that she was paying all of Jason's bills and that she and Jeremy had bought Jason a house. This meant that Jason was no longer living with my in-laws to provide first hand care. We also learned that Olivia was paying Jason a monthly wage for their care! This did not sit well with Stan or me.

These new developments forced us to speak out. We tried to convince Stan's parents to stop paying Jason's way. He was old enough to take care of himself. They needed their money for their **OWN** care. I thought Jason needed some "tough love", but knew he wouldn't change unless he wanted to. His pattern of behavior had been well established since early childhood. It was obvious neither parent could make sound decisions for a safe and secure future.

Decline in Their Condition

Stan and I observed his parents' health going downhill. They often sat in their dark house for days on end with the curtains drawn. Other days, they never got out of bed.

Olivia and Jeremy's neighbor was helping Stan and I keep tabs on his parents. She was concerned and called us saying she could hear Jason screaming at them. According to her, only occasionally would he bring them food from the store and then immediately leave.

Numerous times, Olivia told us she only had coffee and a biscuit to eat all day. With her dementia, Stan and I could never be sure whether what she told us was fact, or forgetfulness. We were left with a big question mark about what was actually happening in their house.

Safety Concerns

My in-laws' neighbor also reported to us that an alarm system had been installed and Jason was locking his parents in the house at night and leaving. If his parents opened the door and wandered outside, the fire department came to shut off the alarm and get them safely back inside.

There was an incident while Stan and I were visiting his parents when Jason instigated a fight between his father and mother. Jeremy became very agitated, had an outburst and threatened Olivia. Now I was afraid for her physical safety.

Stan was angry with his brother for taking advantage of their parents' condition and bleeding them financially. I was afraid the brothers would get in a physical altercation. One, or both, might wind up in the hospital or jail. It seemed wiser to me not to see or communicate with Jason at all. Stan had tried to help Jason in the past by giving him work, providing guidance and setting a good example, but Jason went down a different path. Still, Stan loved him. He was his brother.

I was told by a mutual family friend that Jason said he couldn't wait until his parents were dead. This was certainly not a show of love from a son. It felt like a threat and another cause of concern for their welfare and safety.

Help Rejected

Stan and I were really at a loss. How could we aid my in-laws if they claimed they were "fine" and insisted they didn't need our help? In 2006, Stan and I visited an elder care lawyer for advice. After explaining the situation, we were told we would have to obtain a doctor's statement declaring both parents incapacitated, in order to be granted legal guardianship. This meant Stan's parents would lose all rights to any decision making. Courts are not anxious to do this without very good reason.

I contacted my in-laws' doctor again and he confirmed that both parents had dementia. He said Stan's father was totally incapacitated, but he wasn't sure of the extent of Stan's mother's condition. The doctor said it appeared that Olivia and Jeremy were being taken care of by the other son and he had no proof that the parents' affairs were being mishandled. The doctor was not willing to declare both parents incapacitated.

Contacting the Local Dept. of Human Resources (DHR)

Another few months went by, and it was now 2007. Since it appeared that my in-laws' doctor was not going to help Stan and I secure the care we believed his parents needed, we decided to go another route by contacting the local Department of Human Resources (DHR). I reported what I believed to be financial and physical abuse of my in-laws. We were told that the DHR had a large backlog of cases to investigate, but someone would look into it. Stan and I put our long anticipated vacation out West to see the redwood trees on hold.

At least six years had passed since the first noticeable signs of Stan's parents' difficulties and most likely eight years into their disease. Now, when Stan called his parents, they were typically in bed by 6pm and not answering. We left messages, but it was obvious that they no longer knew how to dial a phone, so communication dwindled. Also, Stan and I felt less welcome at their house. What else could we do? Finally, I put everything in God's hands.

Three months after I had contacted DHR, Stan and I received a phone call back from them stating they had received another report of abuse involving Stan's parents. DHR could not disclose the source or nature of this report to us. We were asked if we still wanted to help Olivia and Jeremy. When Stan and I assented, we were told to be on the alert for a call. We were more than ready to assist, as Stan's parents could no longer help or protect themselves.

During the first DHR visit to my in-laws' home, the social worker was denied access to the house. On the second unannounced visit she was allowed in. The social worker told us that there was food in the refrigerator so she couldn't state that Olivia and Jeremy were not being fed. However, the social worker had not been allowed to speak to my in-laws privately to find out other important care details. On the third visit, the DHR case worker found a drastic decline in Olivia's condition.

Shortly thereafter, I received the call from DHR that Stan and I should come immediately to his parents' house. I left work. We were instructed to move them to the safety of our own home.

DHR had finally been able to question Stan's parents alone. Olivia told them that she was afraid for her life and that Jason was trying to kill her. Stan and I knew that neither parent had been mentally or physically strong enough to stand up to Jason.

If it had not been for DHR's access to the house, and Olivia's cry for help, Stan and I would have been unable to assist them. In searching the house, the police found a stun gun and brass knuckles. We assumed, at the very least, these had been used by Jason to threaten his parents (or worse). Straps on the bed, used to tie them down, had also been discovered. How could a son do this to his parents? Stan and I were horrified.

A Safe Haven

Stan and I brought his parents to our house. We made them comfortable in our bedroom, with a mattress on the floor next to the bed so they wouldn't get hurt if they rolled out at night. We had an on-suite bathroom, with a walk-in shower they could use safely. The DHR social worker came to review the home conditions and assured us all was suitable. I took vacation-time from work.

Olivia, now in a wheelchair, propped up with pillows, was typically in a daze and staring blankly. Jeremy would scold her for not sitting up straight at the table. He didn't understand what was wrong with her. Stan or I had to hold the fork and feed his mother. Sometimes her head sagged into the dinner plate. I started a log of everything the parents ate, including portion sizes and times, took their blood pressure and Olivia's sugar readings twice a day, and attempted to figure out what all the new bottles of prescription medications were for. Olivia had a urinary tract infection which increased her confusion and is usually one of the first things doctors check for.

The Police and Restraining Order

The police, who had accompanied DHR to my in-laws' house when we rescued them, instructed Stan and me to get a Restraining Order (RO) against Jason. We went to the courthouse and completed paperwork explaining Jason's abuse of his parents. After several days, Stan and I had the Restraining Order in hand and felt it was safe enough to return his parents to their home, where they would be in familiar surroundings. A copy of the RO would be served upon Jason.

Accompanied by DHR, we arrived to find that Jason had changed the door locks. We couldn't get back inside. The police and a locksmith were summoned so we could gain access. Three days later, Jason arrived at the house and tried to get in. We were inside. Stan called 911 and reported that Jason had violated the Restraining Order. Now there were criminal charges against him!

Where Do We Go From Here? / Hospice

Stan turned sixty-two at the end of the previous month. Although he had cut back on his construction work, he had planned to continue part time. Now that we were in charge of his parents' care, if Stan worked, almost everything he made would go to pay a caregiver. The best plan of action was for him to assume full care of his parents. In either scenario, we had to adjust to the loss of his income.

The DHR social worker told Stan and me that a dementia patient could be walking one day and be dead within two weeks. Due to Olivia's severely declined state, Hospice care was ordered. Stan needed to be there for his mother to the end. The DHR social worker continued communication with us, a county mental health manager came to evaluate Stan's parents and a Hospice Chaplain arrived.

With Hospice, our personal care, and a new doctor specializing in the elderly, Olivia began to improve dramatically. I had to bathe and dress her myself. DHR had suggested I do this because often a female dementia patient accused a man of sexual abuse, especially while getting a bath. I also did her hair and nails to make her feel and look groomed.

Stan could help his father to the shower and get dressed. Jeremy was still talking and feeding himself, but other than that he needed total assistance.

Review of Medications and Recent Medical History

Stan and I both accompanied his parents to their doctor visits. I used my personal sick time from work. My in-laws' medications needed serious review as they had over 30 prescriptions from different doctors.

There was no medication list with diagnoses, no treatment plan and none of the pills had been sorted into weekly pill containers. It would have been hard for any caregiver to decipher what drugs Stan's parents should have been taking or when to distribute them.

I contacted my in-laws' pharmacy to obtain the history of every prescription, when it had first been ordered, and what treatment each was for. Stan and I were told by the new elder care doctor that Stan's parents were taking numerous drugs that were inappropriate for their conditions. These were immediately discontinued. Even cold tablets could be very detrimental to the dementia patient. Each parent was now down to eight medications daily.

I placed a list on the refrigerator of important contact numbers including doctors, lawyers, Hospice, DHR, and church people. The list also included government benefit numbers, medications with dosages and when they should be administered. I filled Olivia and Jeremy's individually labeled prescription holders weekly.

Stan and I did not know that Jeremy suffered from prolonged post traumatic stress disorder (PTSD). Although we were aware of his WWII ordeal when his Navy destroyer was sunk, we didn't realize Jeremy was now being treated for PTS. After WWII, it may not have been recognized and psychiatric help unavailable at that time.

The discovery of his PTS validated behavioral issues Stan had shared with me from his childhood. All the immediate family members, and especially the children, would have benefitted from that knowledge and from counseling to help them cope with living with someone with severe PTS. It impacted all of them in different ways, Stan running away from home several times beginning in his mid-teens. There were additional behavioral issues, possibly from another disorder.

I never realized that Jeremy had retired at age 45 with 60% disability pay for his PTS. Later, this increased to 80% and finally to the full 100%. I was unaware of the psychiatric care he had been receiving in recent years. To Stan's parents, these things were not to be discussed. They never shared any of this information with us.

Stan and I knew that his father had a drinking problem. Perhaps he was trying to block out recurring nightmares of his ship sinking, half the crew killed by Japanese, or eaten by sharks as they awaited rescue. We also learned that drinking problems may increase the risk of dementia, with those people exhibiting personality changes and explosive behavior.

Stan's father remained on high doses of the drug Depakote for PTS and bi-polar condition; Mirtazapine for major depressive disorder; and Galantamine (Aricept) for dementia.

Olivia's Aricept had been discontinued prior to Stan and I assuming her care and she hadn't received her B12 shot in 3 months due to Jason's negligence. She was taking other medications for dizziness and for depression, saying she was ready for the grave. Some doctors believe that after five years on Aricept, benefits cease and the drug should be discontinued. Other doctors believe it should be continued indefinitely. Olivia's new doctor put her back on Aricept and increased the dosage.

While reviewing my in-laws' paperwork, I found both parents had multiple hospital visits for injuries sustained while under Jason's "care". One document described Olivia's falls in the bath tub, another in the bedroom. Jason had locked them in for the night and left. Olivia couldn't get up, Jeremy was oblivious or unable to assist her, and no one found her until the next morning. She suffered head and back injuries and showed evidence of a previous shoulder fracture. She was now listed as a high fall risk.

Legal Drama-Search and Discovery of Assets

The police, the DHR social worker, a DHR lawyer, a Conservator (appointed by the judge to manage finances and/or daily life due to mental limitations), the Conservator lawyer, the court appointed Guardian ad Litem (appointed to act on my in-laws' behalf), a District Attorney (since it was considered a criminal case), and our previous elder care lawyer were all involved. The myriad of legal terms were new to me as were the roles played and interactions. DHR was often the intermediary between Stan and me and the Conservator.

My in-laws' car was missing and when Stan drove by his brothers' house he saw it parked there. The car had to be recovered because the parents could not easily get into Stan's pick-up truck for trips to the doctor. Stan reported to the police that Jason had taken his parents' vehicle.

Jason was arrested for the theft but was almost immediately released. He proved his parents had given him the title. Several days later, the car was left at my in-laws' house so we were free to use it, although Stan's parents didn't have ownership. The lawyers would have to get that resolved.

Since Stan was providing the daytime care and didn't handle paperwork well, I became the one in charge of the research, discovery and the "proof" that was needed to recover any assets for my in-laws. I was in continuous contact with DHR and the lawyers. I now managed two households of bills and important papers.

At first, Stan was considered Temporary Guardian while legal proceedings to obtain Permanent Guardianship moved forward. Having both parents declared "Incapacitated" by the court involved visiting my in-laws' previous doctor to obtain their medical records, taking them to a neurologist, getting CAT and MRI scans, getting mini-mental evaluations from two different doctors, and having DHR and the police testify to conditions they had found in the home.

While Jeremy's psychiatric records could have been subpoenaed and would have aided us with a full understanding of all the mental issues, the primary goal at the moment was to obtain legal guardianship due to his Alzheimer's disease. We already had that verification. Stan's parents could obviously not make sound decisions as evidenced by the loss of their assets, leaving them destitute and without proper physical care.

I stayed up late at night for weeks going through my in-laws' documents, bills and receipts to figure out what had happened to their money. I turned over the evidence to the lawyers to handle from there. I discovered that in addition to buying Jason a house, his parents had put him on their bank account. Jason used their money for himself to pay for thousands of dollars in house renovations, a new truck, 3 expensive motorcycles, a large work trailer, $10,000 in dental implants, chiropractic visits, a burial crypt, all his food, clothes, furniture, appliances, electric, water, phone, and cable bills, taxes, and several vacations, as well as his "care" salary.

While Jason had been using my in-laws' money to pay his own bills, he had neglected to pay theirs. I had to make calls to prevent the electric and cable in their house from being shut off and pay numerous late charges on their accounts. Jason had also changed my in-laws' home insurance policy into his name. That's how I discovered he had taken ownership of their house as well!

Stan and I had long suspected that Jason was up to no good, but we had no idea of the extent. Besides having his parents sign over all their assets to him, he had them change their wills, naming him and his son as sole beneficiaries. Somehow he had secured a Durable Power of Attorney over his parents after they were already incapacitated and incapable of making these types of decisions.

Jason had been systematically cleaning out my in-laws' bank account. He had set up 22 different bank accounts in his own name, in several different states, in an attempt to hide the money. Stan and I were told by the lawyer that any money across state lines would be nearly impossible to recover. Letters were drawn up and delivered by the lawyers, prohibiting both Jason and his son from any communication with Olivia, Jeremy, Stan or me.

My in-laws only had $2,000 left to their name. Stan and I were now paying his parents' utilities, buying their groceries and personal items, and paying for any non-covered medical expenses and their legal bills.

Due to the severe abuse of my in-laws' funds, Stan and I did not want any fingers potentially pointed at us with questions about spending. Additionally, neither Stan nor I had the time or knowledge to pursue legal matters. The Conservator was assigned to freeze my in-laws' bank account, and to set up a new, secure account for future monies. Going forward, the Conservator got a percent of every bank transaction made on my in-laws' behalf.

Plans for extended long term care were difficult. Olivia and Jeremy had no available funds or assets. Stan and I would have had to place them in the worst facility with an opening. To us, that was not acceptable and left caregiving to us in their home.

Shortly into the initial legal pursuits, Stan was served with a Counter Suit for Malicious Prosecution by Jason. We had to hire yet another lawyer to represent Stan, and more of our personal money went down the drain for his defense. Luckily this lawsuit was quickly thrown out.

During this time, my own parents were confronted by Jason. He knew where they lived and I thought they might become targets of revenge on Stan and me for pursuing the recovery of my in-laws assets. I was afraid for us all: for my in-laws, for my parents, and for Stan and for myself, because I felt Jason was unstable.

Jason and his lawyer tried several tactics to postpone the legal recovery process, claiming Jason was working out of town. Jason's lawyer also filed an Appeal to have the case moved from Probate Court to the Circuit Court. This took several additional months of legal filings, back and forth, before it too was dismissed.

After eight months of delays, the Conservator finally obtained Jason's deposition. Jason admitted gambling away a good portion of his parents' money in casinos. Stan and I also learned from Jason's now fourth ex-wife that he had been using his parents' money to buy drugs and to pay for prostitutes. Stan and I had several character witnesses lined up, willing to testify about Jason's financial misappropriation, threats, bullying, and abusive behavior toward his parents and toward others.

My in-laws' money and many personal belongings of value were long gone and non-recoverable. In addition to Jason swindling his parents' money, his lawyer, who had assisted him in revising the parents' wills, had set up a trust fund for Jeremy with $25,000. Now this lawyer claimed that money was "gone". I filed a Complaint with the State Bar about this lawyer, but was told there was insufficient evidence for them to take action. However, a few years later, the lawyer was tracked down, arrested and disbarred for doing the same thing to other families. Some justice was served, although that money was never recovered.

Loss of Memory and Falling

Neither Olivia nor Jeremy knew where they were, where they lived, what year, month, or day it was. They didn't know day from night and had trouble counting and writing. During the initial mini-mental evaluations (which took place in June of 2006), Stan's mother said it was the fall of 1980. Somehow, she had lost twenty-nine years of her life! She couldn't remember any month or any object shown to her a few minutes earlier. She scored only 16 points out of a possible 30. Less than 23 points indicates cognitive impairment. Stan's father said it was November and the fall. He couldn't remember any year and didn't know where he was. Following is one of the mini-mental exam results.

The Mini-Mental State Exam

Patient _____ Examiner L. Roberts, CMA Date 7-1-09

Maximum	Score	
5	(0)	**Orientation** 1980 ~~Fall~~ Ø mon Ø What is the (year) ~~(season)~~ (date) (day) (month)?
5	(3)	Where are we (state) (country) (town) (hospital) (floor)? Arizona AZ USA ~~Hts~~ Red Store
3	(3)	**Registration** Dog, Cat, Ball Name 3 objects: 1 second to say each. Then ask the patient all 3 after you have said them. Give 1 point for each correct answer. Then repeat them until he/she learns all 3. Count trials and record. Trials _____
5	(3)	**Attention and Calculation** Serial 7's. 1 point for each correct answer. Stop after 5 answers. 7, 14, 21, 28, 35 Alternatively spell "world" backward. ld wor
3	(0)	**Recall** Ask for the 3 objects repeated above. Give 1 point for each correct answer. No
		Language
2	(2)	Name a pencil and watch. ✓
1	(1)	Repeat the following "No ifs, ands, or buts". ✓
3	(2)	Follow a 3-stage command: "Take a paper in your hand, ~~fold it in half~~ and put it on the floor."
1	(1)	Read and obey the following: CLOSE YOUR EYES ✓
1	(1)	Write a sentence.
1	(0)	Copy the design shown.
30	**16**	

I love mom
son

Total Score 16   <23 Cognitive Impairment
ASSESS level of consciousness along a continuum _____
Alert (Drowsy) Stupor Coma

Olivia spent a good portion of the night squirreling through her bedroom closet searching for things she believed were lost - keeping Stan and I awake. I got little sleep and went to work drained. It was exhausting. At least Stan could cat nap, as his parents did, during the day.

Occasionally, Olivia would fall getting out of bed. Stan would rush to their room, pick his mother up. After one such dead weight lift, Stan hurt his back and was in severe pain. He required major surgery to remove bone splinters and have plates, screws and cadaver bone fused to his spine and neck. This required an in-hospital stay, with me picking up total parental care duty, along with caring for

Stan while he recovered. He was advised not to lift anything heavy in the future.

After another of Olivia's falls it was all I could do, being of the same build and weight as she, to lift her back onto the side of the bed. After that, Stan and I resolved to prevent any injuries to his mother or us.

Some Health Improvement

After three months of care, Olivia was walking again and could feed herself. Hospice was cancelled, although Olivia still needed assistance with everything else. She had no comprehension of happenings.

My concentration focused on feeding the family healthy, home-cooked meals and continuing to help my mother-in-law with her personal care. During the day, I went to my full-time job; Stan cared for his parents. Nights and weekends, I assisted or took over full duty.

In the fall, Stan and I took my in-laws on an outing to the Botanical Gardens, each of us pushing a wheelchair. We all enjoyed getting out of the house to sunshine, fresh air and beautiful flowers. It was a short escape from all the problems we were facing.

Stan's father was starting the last stage of the disease and shuffling his feet. He was having greater difficulty walking. He was using a cane which we tried to discourage because he tended to put all his weight to one side, increasing the risk of tripping or tipping over. He was resistant to using a walker - it "wasn't manly".

Care Aids

In addition to bars inside and outside the shower, Stan and I bought a transfer seat to make it easier to move his mother in and out of the bathtub. A hand held shower wand was also very useful. I purchased bars for the side of the toilet to help the parents sit and stand and a bar for the side of the bed to help them pull up on.

I disposed of all throw rugs to prevent tripping, but left one rug outside the bathtub. It was rubber backed and wouldn't slip. Both parents already had walkers and wheelchairs due to previous falls and physical limitations.

Stan and I purchased a bed alarm and baby monitors so we'd know when Olivia was getting up during the night, but the alarm just kept us from sleeping. It would go off every time his mother moved off the sensor pad. We eventually packed it away.

When either parent seemed agitated, Stan and I utilized aromatherapy, burning vanilla and lavender candles for their calming effect. I bought a sound machine with settings for a rain forest, birds and the ocean –anything that might help soothe them. Music seemed most effective in mood-altering, especially music from the 1940's which they still remembered. Sometimes we listened to soft classical music.

Hallucinations and Psychosis

My mother-in-law was hallucinating a lot at this time and claimed someone was spying on her and Jeremy. She said she saw lights in the bedroom at night. Stan and I told her these were reflections in the mirror. Stan and I learned that people with dementia are usually disturbed by glare, especially from windows or mirrors. That was probably the reason my in-laws had previously shut their curtains and sat in the dark.

I'm sure a lot of Olivia's fear stemmed from the ordeal and confusion with DHR, the police, Hospice, social workers, shuffling between our house and hers, different doctors, lawyers, court, Jason's threats and the Restraining Order.

Stan and I learned that Jason had been forwarding my in-laws' phone to his house, recording our calls. He knew everything we had previously been saying to Stan's parents and that's how he had been able to keep one step ahead of us. Now even Stan and I were feeling somewhat paranoid!

In the middle of one night, Olivia started yelling that she was having a heart attack and dying. Stan called 911 and his mother was transported to the hospital. Olivia was kept overnight, numerous tests were performed and she was examined by five different doctors. We were told there was nothing wrong with his mother, other than her dementia and acute delirium! These psychotic episodes could not be ignored however. She might actually be having a heart attack or other major health issue in the future.

Daily Life

Stan was searching for activities to share with his parents while he sat with them during the day. I bought what I thought would be a very simple puzzle for Olivia and Jeremy to work on, but neither parent was capable of matching more than one or two pieces together. Stan wound up completing the puzzle himself.

Jeremy used to enjoy reading old western novels. I took Olivia to the library, where we found a few books on tape that she and Jeremy could listen to.

Mostly, Stan's parents were content to sit and watch television or say a few words to each other during the day. Both could still follow very simple, single instructions.

I bought DVD's they could watch. These included movies on our national parks, sunrise across the planet, and ocean wonders. These were calming, rested the mind and renewed an appreciation of the beauty of nature.

Stan's father had nose drops to help with his breathing, but if he wasn't watched closely he would put the drops in his coffee. Occasionally, pills would wind up on the floor. We had to be sure to witness the pills getting into their mouths and swallowed.

Stan prepared his parents lunch, fixed things in the house and did the laundry. He also searched through the garage and attic to find out what was there, disposing of unnecessary items.

Every night during the week when I arrived from work, Stan would drive to our own house, a half hour away, to pick up our mail. Then he drove another half hour back to his parents' house for the night. During that time I was in charge of care.

Luckily, my in-laws improved enough to understand what a will was and who Stan and I were. Their wills were revised to the originals. Distributions to Jason and his son were excluded.

Search for In-Home Caregivers

Hospice provided Stan and me with a list of potential caregivers and I spent a lot of time calling, interviewing and trying various people out. We could not afford to pay anyone full-time, as all their expenses were coming out of our pocket. Our bank account was taking a big hit, but Stan needed respite now and again from day-long parental care.

Most caregivers wanted guarantees of a full week's work for some extended period of time, not just a few hours on occasion. That made it difficult to find qualified and available people to give Stan a break.

It also seemed that Stan's mother did not like most of the caregivers because they didn't pay her enough attention or talked too much about themselves. She even ordered one of them to leave. The cheapest caregiver I found charged $12/hour per person, two people, $24/hour. Most were not anxious to clean house or prepare meals. I really think they just wanted to sit.

There was also an issue of smoking. Stan was highly allergic to smoke and his parents and I were bothered by it as well. Even if the caregiver smoked outside, it remained on clothing. I had to add that to the list of questions in the caregiver screening process.

Those times my in-laws were left alone with a caregiver in their house, I carried my jewelry in the car. I didn't want to invite temptation. I had already seen my in-laws' possessions disappear, and that, by the hands of their own son!

Stan and I submitted our suggested caregiver rate to the Conservator. It required court approval. At the hearing, the judge approved a rate of $9.50/hour for both parents for an 18 hour day, not 24 hours. This rate was established since Stan's parents had little money. It would be a long time until their funds could build up to pay the going rate. Potential caregivers had to accept this pay or Stan and I would have to cover the difference.

It was eight months later before enough funds were accumulated in the new account, reimbursing Stan and me for money spent on my in-laws' behalf up to that point. Thereafter, I submitted weekly expense reports to the Conservator which were reviewed and paid the following month.

Stan and I were very careful with his parents' expenditures. We were allowed to purchase everyday necessities such as food, household items and clothes. If anything additional was needed, a special petition and approval from the court was required.

Support Options

Actual physical or informational support was provided by various people in different ways. This help came from neighbors, friends, my mother, DHR, Hospice, the Alzheimer's Association, doctors, lawyers, community programs, other caregivers and our churches.

I contacted Meals on Wheels to find out if Olivia and Jeremy would qualify for their program. I was told that Meals on Wheels could not provide meals because my in-laws were not alone – Stan and I were there taking care of them.

Another neighbor was active in a local senior center which provided meals to the participants. On days when meals were left over, this neighbor brought food for Olivia and Jeremy. This saved Stan and me some money.

I discovered that my own parents' church had a charity program which provided short-term assistance to those facing difficult circumstances. I submitted a request for aid, describing my in-laws' destitution and Stan's and my need for care relief. The request was reviewed and approved by the church committee. Through this program, Stan and I were able to secure two paid caregivers for my in-laws on the weekends for a period of three months. Now we could go home and maintain our property. It was a huge relief and savings for us, personally.

Despite the various aid sources I had uncovered, it seemed my life was totally consumed in the care of my in-laws: keeping them alive, trying to improve their health with good food and the right medications, and monitoring all the legal proceedings. It was overwhelming trying to juggle my full-time career with caregiving and a marriage.

Combative Behavior

Stan's father was spending a good portion of the day in bed, or just sitting in a chair. He was peeing all over the bathroom floor which meant Stan was endlessly cleaning.

Sometimes, Jeremy refused to get out of bed. Other times, he wouldn't cooperate getting bathed or dressed. My birthday was especially upsetting to me. Jeremy refused to get dressed though Stan and I were taking both parents with us to my parents' house to celebrate. We did finally get Jeremy ready, but we arrived at my parents' home hours late. I began to understand that my schedule and time were no longer my own.

Lack of Available Care Facilities

About four months into our caregiving, we decided we should apply for Aid and Attendance benefits for Stan's father and place him in the local Veterans' home. In order to get any financial aid, the patient must have less than $80,000 in the bank, including any stocks or bonds. It does not include the value of your home. Jeremy qualified. We would still have to pay about $100/day out of pocket for his care. I completed paperwork for his admittance. This would free up Stan and me to concentrate on the care of his mother. We waited and waited for months, but the only response from the VA was that Jeremy was still on the list. They could give us no indication when there might be an opening. The facility had only 100 beds in total, with many veterans trying to get in. Also, there were **few spots for those with memory issues.**

Mother-in-Laws Letters

Around this time, which was eight months into our caregiving, my mother-in-law began writing letters to us and to document her thoughts so that she could re-read them later on when she might not remember. She had regained many faculties, was writing again legibly and was aware of the depth of financial and physical abuse that had occurred. The following are her words.

> *"Help me to understand the reason for this time of heartache. I trust in you, O my God. I beg you to forgive my enemy and show him the way back to you. Bless the efforts of Stan and Carissa."*

> *"Is there no end to this nightmare? There doesn't seem to be an end in sight. We continue to be*

drained of all of our funds – as well as any assets. This house is still in Jason's name – our car – numerous other property that belongs to us. Why has he not been required to return them? We are just two old people. I pray that Jason will face the heartache he caused the family and ask God's forgiveness. I wonder if he faces some of the things he did – the suffering he caused – all the women he married and took advantage of. Dad and I loved him so dearly, and still do for that matter. May God forgive me for my failure in raising him right. I must close my heart now, it's too much to bear."

"I am at a loss. Who can I turn to – where can I go? I wanted to do the right thing – to have the right attitude – to pray the right way. I hurt to see Dad's torture, to know I can't lift that pain and heartache off him. I feel I have failed miserably. What can I do to make up? I beat myself with the knowledge that my actions in not dealing with Jason as I should have caused so much pain and sorrow. I trusted him. Please forgive me for not dealing with him as I should have. I have reached the end of my road. I pray for your guidance dear God. I am weak and without your help I can do nothing. I am lost, beaten and afraid."

"Jeremy needs me. I cannot just drop him at this point. He would be there for me and I want to be there for him. How can I maintain my sanity?"

"The only thing that seems important is the continuation of the legal time, without an end or resolution of the problem. I'm of no importance in this matter except to stay alive so that what small pensions we have will continue to be received for

payment of the lawyers' fees. I am tired. I do not want to be a burden on my family. What can I do? I try to keep a sense of humor – to stay busy. I pray a lot. Am I weak in my faith? I'll try harder. Jeremy is better off not being aware of what is happening. Help me not to get discouraged and downhearted."

"I find it hard to quit. I always thought that horror stories would have an ending – this one doesn't. It seems to grow worse as time passes. I know that everyone is as tired of this as I am. How much longer can it go on? How much more can a person endure? The burden is heavy. I beg for help. I am trying to control my desperation."

"Dad and I had a good life. We worked hard and saved what we could. So many things cannot be recovered. How could this happen? Daddy and I are left with nothing. May God forgive Jason and the people who helped him destroy me and Daddy. I can't figure out what I'm missing. I want to understand my situation and find a way to better it. I don't know how to begin. I don't know what to do. I desperately need help. I cannot get a job – and if by chance I do get the house back and am able to sell it – it won't be enough to last me more than a very short time. I remember enough to know that expenses have to be no greater than income. Do you have any suggestions? Sorry to put this load on you, but I must find a way out. I didn't know things could get worse – but they have!! Jason is pulling all tricks to delay settling this case, hoping that given enough time I will die before it's settled. He has given nothing back to me – things he took that his Dad and I bought and paid for – the funds we

saved to provide for this time of our life. I am trying to hold my head up. I am grateful that I have a place to live. I try not to dwell on the situation, but it is hard to accept. I know I'm putting a hardship on my family. I worked and never thought I would have to be dependent on someone else for my living. I do not understand how Jason is able to get by law enforcement. There seems to be no end to what he can get by with. I am happy with my home, the love and care I'm given by my family, and by God and His angels who are ever with me."

It is easy to feel her heartbreak, utter torment and devastation when she realized she had been betrayed. The only thing we could do was to reassure her that she needn't worry; we would handle the problems and she didn't have to go back to work. We would take care of her financially, physically and legally.

While her cognitive abilities had greatly improved from the time we first began providing care, the neurologist explained to my husband and I that this improvement was temporary. He expected my mother-in-law to begin a gradual permanent decline within the next six months. The following is a graph depicting his analogy of the progression of her dementia. From the time of her first test, she had drastically declined during the lack of proper care from Jason. Under our care she had much improved, but would soon begin the descent until death, if she did not die from something else prior to that.

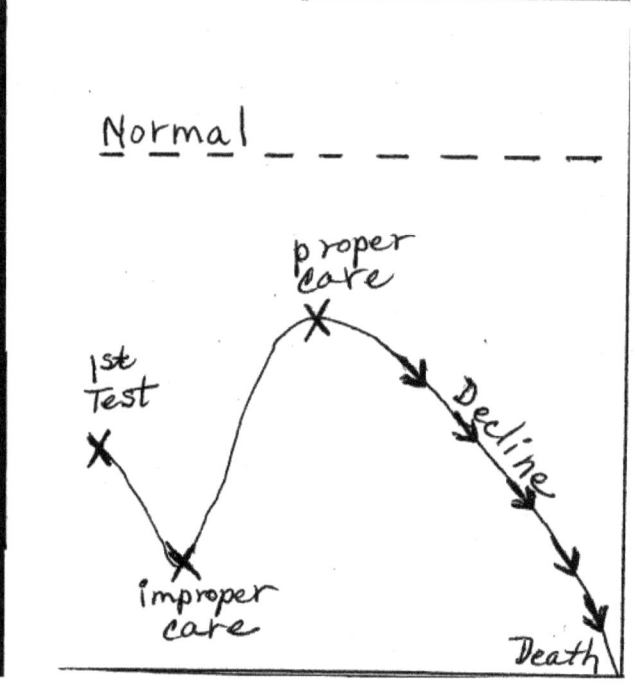

Father-in-Law's Final Days

After ten months in our care, Stan's father fell in the driveway and was taken to the hospital. He had broken his hip. The doctor said the fall was actually due to an atrial fibrillation attack (arrhythmia - too fast, too slow, or irregular heartbeat causing poor blood flow). I stayed with Jeremy at the hospital; Stan stayed with his mother at home. But Stan brought her to visit Jeremy every day. Jeremy still remembered Olivia and asked about her often.

With the dementia, certain things would be remembered and others would not. Sometimes they would be remembered one minute, gone the next, then return later. We were on a constant roller coaster anticipating my in-laws' abilities at any given moment.

Jeremy could not remember his fall or that his hip was broken. Any rehab efforts proved useless. As I sat near the foot of his bed, his biggest concern was whether his feet smelled when his socks were removed. I got a chuckle out of that!

The social workers at the hospital tried to assist Stan and me to arrange future care for his father. The local VA facility was contacted again, but still, no openings. The next closest VA facility with an opening was 2-1/2 hours away. We did not want to ship Stan's father there and rarely be able to visit. We really were at a loss about what to do, other than bring him home, bedridden.

Shortly thereafter, Stan got a call from the doctor at the hospital, saying there was nothing else they could do to help Jeremy. He continued to have atrial fibrillation attacks and was going into heart failure. Stan agreed that his father should be moved to "comfort care". This meant taking Jeremy off all his regular medications, providing pain relief, and piping in some soft classical music to keep him calm.

We visited Jeremy that day in the hospital. He did not seem conscious, but became agitated when we rubbed his arm. The nurse said we could only hold his hand because he was in pain. Jeremy died early the next morning from cardiac arrest, respiratory and congestive heart failure.

Stan called the Conservator to inform him that his father had passed away. It was also a necessary courtesy to inform Jason that his father had died, allowing him the privilege of paying last respects. Through the lawyers, Jason was told that he could attend the funeral as long as he didn't speak to us and didn't cause a disruption. Several police cruisers were stationed outside the funeral home for our protection and ready to remove Jason should there be any trouble. The police told us afterwards that Jason had driven by, but didn't stop. I assume once Jason saw the police, he didn't want to risk being arrested. We were able to get through the memorial service in peace, but looking over our shoulders the whole time.

This year was so painful. We realized the abuse Stan's parents had suffered, were overwhelmed by the legal issues, and came to experience firsthand, what it meant to have dementia and be totally incapacitated.

Short Term Memory Loss

Olivia could not remember that Jeremy had died. This was incomprehensible to Stan and me. They had been married for 63 years! For a long time, if anyone asked Olivia about Jeremy, she said he was in a nursing home, out of state. Other times, she would say he had gone out, but was going to return home shortly. I think she just believed that because she didn't see him around. She did not remember him going to the hospital, seeing him there, or being at his funeral.

A book I read said not to tell a person with dementia that their spouse had died, but Olivia said she wanted to know the truth no matter what. Stan and I were torn about whether to say anything to her which might cause her to get depressed over and over, or to fabricate some other story.

Stan continued to tell his mother of Jeremy's passing and she did not seem bothered by it, other than to be annoyed that she could not remember such an important thing – and which thankfully, was quickly forgotten by her again. Maybe each dementia patient reacts differently to this knowledge and depends on the stage in their disease, but this was our experience with my mother-in-law.

A New Home

The legal battle was finally coming to a conclusion. The lawyers felt the best approach was to recover the house and car and forget about pushing for criminal prosecution of Jason. The latter would have delayed the legal process and cost us a lot more money and time. Olivia might die before anything was resolved.

If we proceeded with the criminal case it would be brought before a Grand Jury and would involve a lengthy investigation. It would also require extensive questioning of Olivia by the police. We believed this would be traumatic for her and the questioning fruitless. Stan and I agreed to recover the car and house and move on with our lives as best we could.

Stan and I had been away from our own home a whole year. We decided it was time to move his mother there with us. I worked up the expected monthly and annual expenditures which were presented to the Conservator and the court for approval. It was more economically feasible to keep his mother at home under our care versus placing her in a facility.

The court approved the sale of my in-laws' home. We had a yard sale and put up a sign advertising the house. Immediately, we had three offers, one of which we accepted. The Conservator handled the legalities of the closing. Within a month, Stan and I packed up the household belongings and we physically moved everything to our home truckload by truckload. One of our large downstairs rooms became a bedroom for Olivia. Her other possessions were put in storage in our shed and garage.

A Short Break for Us

Stan and I decided we needed a short break. It had been a long haul and stressful with caregiving, DHR, police, lawyers, his father's death and the move. The Court now increased the caregiving allowance to $12/hour but would only pay for <u>12 hours</u> a day. They claimed Olivia would be sleeping during the night and wouldn't require supervision. This did not take into account a dementia patient's "sundowning" symptoms. They are often up at night, more agitated and wandering and still require considerable care. If Stan and I were to utilize a caregiver, we would have to pay for the night hours out of our pocket.

During our break, the caregiver stayed with Olivia in our house. Upon our return, Stan's mother told us that the caregiver had gone through our personal things and that the caregiver had been hitting the liquor supply. Stan and I believed there was at least some truth to his mothers' claim. The caregiver said several items had been "broken" and they were now gone. As a result, Stan and I came to believe we couldn't trust others.

We Move Again

At this point, Stan and I could have placed Olivia in a nice care facility, but the proceeds from the sale of her house would cover less than two years of care. We had no idea how many years she might continue to live with the disease. Her condition had actually improved! So, we decided to take the money from the house sale and purchase a manufactured home. We would put it on my adjoining property and stay there with her. We had to wait for approval from the court to move forward. This was a major investment of her money.

There were pros and cons to our decision. Living in a house other than our own prevented any caregiver's pilfering or stealing our personal information. The bedrooms in the manufactured home were all on the same floor, and Stan's mother would be more comfortable and less confused with all of her own possessions around her. It also allowed Stan and me to spend an occasional night alone in our house, provided we could find a trusted sitter to stay with his mother.

The con of this arrangement was: Stan and I had to continue maintaining two properties, I had to clean two houses, and mow four acres. But for now, this seemed the best option.

Soon, the court signed off on the manufactured home purchase and it was transported to my property. We moved in Olivia's belongings and set up the second bedroom and bath with our things. We repurposed wood, Stan, my son and the church deacon building a ramp for easy access into the home for the time when Olivia's condition might worsen. DHR came again to inspect and approve the new living arrangement.

Mental Effect of the Incapacitation Ruling

Olivia was extremely sensitive to being ruled "incapacitated" but she was able to retain some dignity keeping her household belongings. This way, she did not feel like she had lost everything. She had lost her rights, lost her independence and privacy, lost her memory and ability to do most things. Any valuable jewelry, precious personal mementos and various other family keepsakes had been taken from her. Stan and I tried to soften the blow, by explaining that had she not been declared mentally incompetent, nothing at all would have been recovered. At least now she had a home in her name (albeit under the Conservator's control).

At one point, the lawyers asked Olivia why she had signed everything over to Jason. She replied that he was her son and she had trusted him. She didn't know what she was signing. The only good thing about Olivia having dementia was that she almost immediately forgot that sorrow and abuse.

When my mother-in-law's driver's license came up for renewal, Stan and I decided she should get a non-driver's photo ID. Even though we had recovered her car, my mother-in-law knew she could never drive again. Since Stan became her "personal chauffeur", the non-driving ID became acceptable, rather than another right taken away from her.

Day-to-Day Life

Things were gradually unpacked and we settled in the new home. For Stan and me, it was much easier returning to our property. However, we still felt quite isolated from everything and everyone due to the demands of providing full care.

We all welcomed being in the peace of country living. Here Olivia could sit outside enjoying trees and flowers. Most importantly, she was away from the scene of her abuse. This was a happy time for us all.

Animals became an important part of Olivia's recovery. Stan and I placed a birdfeeder outside his mother's bedroom window. She could watch the birds during the day. There was also a feeder where she could see the birds while she sat at the dinner table. Stan loved birds too, and he began making bird calls. His mother would answer with the sound of a dove or owl; the two of them creating a game of it.

Stan and I rescued a baby deer that had been abandoned by its mother on our property. The doe required 8-10 bottles of goat's milk a day and she would come up on our porch to be fed. Holding its bottle for feeding was something Olivia really enjoyed. Olivia could watch from the deck when Stan and I played with the doe in our yard or when it followed us around. We could pet and brush it. It was thrilling to watch as our "Doedy" grew and learned to jump over the creek and run figure 8's. She didn't "come" on demand, but often just appeared, sneaking up on us in the dark of night to say hello, then disappearing back into the woods. Olivia helped gather acorns to feed her as she grew older.

We had a pile of sand in the yard, preparing to pour a garage footer. Doedy liked to jump and play in it, like a child in a sandbox. Eventually, she was adopted by 5 others, their young, and several buck. The herd would come nightly to drink from our creek and eat corn from a bin we put out for them. A year later, Doedy brought her first

offspring for us to see. This was such an educational and inspirational experience for all of us to share. Doedy still stops by occasionally to visit her home turf. Just recently she appeared, two new babies in tow, parading them past us to admire. Stan and I are back to gathering apples and acorns from the yard to leave her as treats.

In addition to enjoying our wildlife, Olivia treasured short visits from friend's grandchildren. Five year olds were full of life and entertaining; and more on her mental level.

Stan and I had muscadines and a large vegetable garden in our backyard. Olivia loved going outside with Stan to pick grapes and snap peas in a large pot for me to cook. We took her to a blueberry farm where she sat in a chair in the field. There, she picked and ate blueberries to her hearts content. Each of us managed to have a full bucket of berries to bring home for some delicious desserts and blueberry pancakes.

Olivia was now granted a small "allowance" each month from the Conservator's account to do with as she pleased. Stan opened a bank account in both he and his mothers name. We managed the money and balanced the checkbook. Olivia could now buy a trinket for herself, or pay for her lunch out. It was a big boost to her morale. Additionally, she could buy small gifts for birthdays and for Christmas. The remainder of the money was kept for emergency.

Olivia still heard and saw things that weren't there. She frequently said someone was knocking on her door, call out and say "come in". She talked about "midgets" jumping on her bed at night. Stan told her they were coming to party, having a good time, don't be fearful.

Olivia wanted her privacy in the bathroom, but we could not leave her alone. There were one or two incidents when she turned on the shower water and left the door open, resulting in a flooded floor. We again assisted by turning the water on and off, and helping her get in and out of the shower safely. Olivia had a shower seat to sit on and rubber backed mats to prevent slipping.

Olivia liked to spend the day in her bedroom, organizing and re-organizing drawers and boxes. Sitting in the living room provided Stan and me a direct line of sight into his mother's bedroom. Sometimes, she kept busy pulling all the artificial flowers out of an arrangement. Then she would try to put them back. Other times, she pulled all the artificial flower petals off and left a mess on the floor. While still keeping an eye on his mother, Stan could often search on the internet or play computer games during the day.

My husband tried to keep his mother entertained and have some fun. Sometimes, she would go along with the kidding, but other times it was totally lost on her or she would get upset. On her better days, they drove in the car. Stan would sing to music from the 1960's. On one of his favorite songs, "Let Me Show You Where It's At" by the Dave Clark Five, Stan would sing the first four lines and was able to teach his mother to respond with the last five words: ….the name of the game is "I like it like that".

Every Sunday, a couple from Olivia's church came to the house to share the homily and give her communion. They provided for her spiritually for years. If they were away or sick, another couple took their place. All of them became like family to us.

Olivia was now in the eleventh year since Stan and I knew something was wrong. This disease could still continue for many more years.

After working at my full-time job during the weekdays, my typical Saturday was spent cleaning, doing the laundry, cooking in advance for the coming week, mowing both properties and watching Olivia. After the church people left on Sunday, I prepared dinner then went to my parents' house for the remainder of the day to assist them. Such was my life for the next several years.

A favorite past time for Olivia, and short break for Stan, was having the church lady take her to Hobby Lobby to buy beads to string. More often than not, everyone else had to do the project because Olivia was no longer able and could only watch.

Olivia sewed and quilted for years, but she could no longer do either. Her "sewing" now consisted of playing with the supplies, fingering loose buttons and sorting pieces of fabric to feel the material.

I assigned Olivia the duty of cleaning her room. Although her cleaning was a tiny sweep of the dust cloth over a portion of one dresser, and I always had to do a proper dusting and vacuum, she felt needed with her contribution.

Years earlier, my mother-in-law enjoyed painting simple art pieces. Now, when I asked her to draw something (a flower or a tree), she stared at the paper, bewildered.

To me, Olivia seemed self-centered. She would make demands of Stan and me about all the things she wanted. She wanted flowers for the deck, she wanted a butterfly bush in the yard, she wanted the curtains changed in her room, she wanted a picture framed and hung. All her "wants" meant something else for Stan or me to do. And it meant further exhaustion for both of us. Sometimes, Olivia could be side-tracked or Stan and I could at least delay the request until a more convenient time.

To me, Olivia also seemed vain, standing in front of a magnifying mirror in her bedroom for hours, plucking hair from her face. Maybe it was just a way for her to pass the time, but I wound up taking the mirror and the tweezers away because she was gauging holes around her eyebrows and chin which could get infected.

Olivia enjoyed sitting outside on the front deck when the weather was nice. Now when she wanted to go out, she often said the door was locked. When Stan or I tried it, it was open. Olivia had forgotten how to open the door.

Breaking and Losing Things

Things got broken. Olivia could open the patio umbrella but not close it. The pull cord tore. The lamp knobs in her bedroom were broken, as well as the blinds. When Olivia tried to force the washing machine door open before the cycle was complete, the handle broke off. Her walker brakes broke because she held the brakes on constantly while trying to walk. Olivia no longer knew how to use the microwave or the electric can opener. Even pushing the button to turn on the vacuum or lower the handle was a challenge. She could no longer operate equipment properly.

More and more things were becoming "lost", including Olivia's hearing aids. She would frequently accuse Stan and me of taking them. Since she could not remember where she put them, Stan and I searched everywhere. Sometimes we would find one hearing aid under the bed, another in a dresser drawer, or one in a shoe and one in an artificial flower pot. Another was shoved in the guts of a chair. We finally found it a year after Olivia died.

Sometimes she took the batteries out of her aids and put the aids in her ears, so of course, she couldn't hear. If she didn't have her aids in, we wound up shouting. In addition to her needing them to hear, wearing the aids was extremely important to help with her walking and balance.

Stan and I put a plan in place to get Olivia's hearing aids separated from her before she went to bed at night and then give them back in the morning. Even doing that, one went missing while she was in her room during the day. Luckily, she had an old pair to wear as backup.

As Olivia liked playing with her jewelry, a good portion of her costume earrings became lost – or at least one earring of the pair would disappear. I was continually trying to find and rematch them because she still liked to "dress up" when going out or if someone was coming to visit.

Physical Improvement but Increase in Memory Loss

Olivia had increased her walking to 10 laps up and down the ramp to the house each day. Physically, she was doing much better. Often Stan and I walked with her to get our own exercise and to be sure she was safe and didn't fall.

Despite her physical improvement, Olivia's memory continued to decline. She could no longer remember where the light switches were and go from one side of the room to the other in search of them.

Stan and I assigned his mother table setting duty. For a time she managed to do this, but later in the disease she forgot what we had asked of her. After 4 or 5 requests, she would disappear into her room and reappear an hour later, just when we were ready to eat.

Ultimately, Olivia no longer remembered where the plates and utensils were. She would search through every cabinet and drawer in the kitchen. When she finally thought she had set the table, we might have one fork, or a plate but no cups. I added the missing tableware without comment.

Short Excursions Outside of the Home

It was almost impossible to keep to a timetable, or predict the mood or emergency we might face trying to get out the door at any given time. Stan and I always had to allow at least three hours for Olivia to get ready. We learned not to schedule appointments before 11:00 AM. Sometimes that wasn't possible and we'd have to get Olivia up at 4:30 in the morning to make an 8:00 doctor's visit.

Stan took his mother to her monthly retiree group luncheons, but she remembered no one. The group gradually dwindled to two or three attendees. Gatherings were cut to once every quarter and then to twice a year. The other retirees were very sweet to Olivia but anyone could see it pained all. They had worked with her for years when her mind had been sharp. Now they didn't know how to talk to her. Olivia just kept introducing herself and asking who they were.

I continued to take Olivia to the hair dresser. The time came when she could no longer sit for three hours for a perm. Eventually, she got her hair cut every other month and let her hair dry naturally. It was left uncurled because she couldn't manage a curling iron and might burn herself. I wasn't there during the week days to curl it. Once in awhile, Stan gave it his best shot, but he wasn't much of a lady's hair stylist.

Stan also took his mother to a Balance Class twice a week. The Balance Class helped teach the participants to balance after standing up, to walk properly, to sit down and stand up again. It was especially beneficial in teaching how to get up after a fall: roll on your side, bend the knees, get up onto the knees and finally stand. It was important to wear good support shoes with non-skid soles or sneakers. Stan and I practiced the balance exercises at home with Olivia as well.

After six months Olivia quit. She could no longer comprehend instructions. She said there was a new "drill sergeant" leading the class and it was "no fun". Stan and I couldn't force her to participate.

Tai Chi classes were also offered at this location. This was way beyond Olivia's capabilities. It might be something to consider for your loved one if they are still mobile, have good balance and can follow instructions.

Issues with Eating

One of the biggest challenges Stan and I had was with Olivia's eating. She gained a lot of weight because she had lost all sense of being full. She would continually eat yet insist she was "starving". Years earlier, she had been on insulin shots for her diabetes, but under our care, she improved to the point of being able to take pills.

Olivia couldn't remember when she had last eaten and so would insist she hadn't eaten at all. Sometimes she would sneak food to her room, to eat later. Stan and I found empty containers in the refrigerator and empty boxes of crackers in the kitchen cabinet, so it wasn't immediately apparent that his mother had been eating things up.

Olivia raided the refrigerator when Stan or I were out of sight. One day she ate a whole package of sliced ham, two apples, several slices of cheese and three yogurts in a half an hour while I was cleaning elsewhere in the house. We had only eaten our dinner an hour earlier.

Now, Stan took his mother's weight every day. We tried to monitor her food intake very closely. I measured and pre-packaged her portions of cereal for dispensing every morning. All of us started on a Heart Healthy diet.

A book I read concerning dementia eating issues suggested putting a lock on the refrigerator door. Instead, I stored all the food at our house and just brought the food for a specific meal to the manufactured home. That way, the refrigerator remained free of temptation for my mother-in-law. With these changes, Olivia lost the unneeded weight and her diabetes improved so significantly that she no longer needed any medication. Olivia's doctor was as amazed by this as we were.

The Toll on Us

The years of full-time care continued. There were so many challenges in dealing with this disease, challenges neither Stan nor I imagined when we began to help. One often hears about changes in persons with dementia, but rarely about the effects on the people taking care of them.

I now felt as if I had aged 30 years and was as old as the parents were. I was on their schedules, their life-style, and dealt with their issues. Olivia continued to be awake a good portion of the night, slamming drawers in her bedroom or bathroom. The slightest noise woke me up as I "slept" in a state alert and ready. I was awakened at least every two hours and had difficulty getting back to sleep. It was similar to having a newborn, but usually they develop a good sleep pattern within several months. These sleep issues went on for years. Stan and I both listened with one ear monitoring, waiting for the sound of a crash, meaning his mother had fallen.

I experienced periods of depression, mourning the loss of a previous life. I missed the freedom, the spur of the moment pleasure of going out on a dinner or movie date with Stan, time together with friends, or planning a vacation. Because there was never time to watch the news, I felt very disconnected from world events. And, of course, it was devastating to witness the impact of this disease on a loved one.

Stan and I had absolutely no privacy. Intimacy was virtually nil because I was too exhausted to even think about the possibility.

Everything revolved around Stan's mother. She always came first – which is not a great thing for any marriage. At one point, I told Stan I felt like he was married to his mother, not me. It was hard not to be resentful or feel that she had robbed Stan and me of our closeness.

And then there was the guilt: guilt that I wanted my life back; guilt that I wanted a few moments alone with my husband; guilt that I wanted a few moments to myself; guilt that I still had my mind and body when the parents had lost theirs; guilt that even with all we had done, we should be doing more for them; guilt that we were going to take a 5 day vacation and leave the parents in the care of a sitter. Did I deserve to be happy and enjoy life when our parents could not? Could I allow myself that luxury? I struggled with these emotions for a long time.

Caregiving had taken over my life. Luckily, my husband and I were both committed to this cause and our marriage was strong enough to survive. We knew the caregiving would not last forever, although there were times when it certainly felt like it would.

Whenever Olivia lashed out in her frustration, I got upset, aggravating my mitral valve issue. With my heart murmur, increased palpitations and arrhythmia worsening, I often had to separate myself from her. Without health or sanity, I would be useless to the family.

My boss knew I was attending to everyone's needs except my own. One Christmas he gave me a gift certificate for a massage and pedicure. It was a real treat and I forced myself to take two hours off to enjoy it.

I had heard stories about caregivers who died before their loved one. They died because they neglected their own health, mentally and physically. I began a self-help program on the treadmill for 30 minutes every other day, and watched my diet. Reading became a way to relax before bed.

Over the years of caregiving, Stan had five eye surgeries to repair detached retina, a cancer scare, several biopsies, an emergency room visit, and a major spine and neck surgery. The bone fragments in his neck and spine were pressing on nerves, causing a loss of feeling in hands and arms. It could have become permanent. Lastly, both hands developed Dupuytrens Contracture, a condition causing tendons in the hands to draw up and harden. Fingers curl in and the hands become claw-like. He required surgery to prevent that eventuality.

Again, I had to take sick and vacation time to meet these needs. I asked "Lord, how will I take care of four people?" At that point, I thought Stan's mother would have to go in a home, but Stan did well with each surgery. He rebounded quickly and resumed the care of his mother.

Personally, I had foot and walking issues: almost constant pain from Plantar Fasciitis, and repeated Morton's neuromas. Several foot surgeries were necessary and special orthotic shoes. I had severe trouble with menopause, including constant hot flashes. My mitral valve issue was getting worse and all the stress caused it to regurgitate fluid into my lungs. Infection!

Additional testing revealed I was born with arterial deformities. This, in combination with my cardiac arrhythmia, was limiting blood flow and might cause me to pass out. It required close monitoring now. Next, I developed osteoarthritis in my feet, hips and hands. My fingers locked up in the morning. At night, I couldn't get comfortable in bed with the pain in my hip. Sometimes, after my surgeries, I spent a day at my house in peace and quiet so I could recover. Having a place of escape was a plus while providing caregiving elsewhere.

It was difficult for Stan and me to maintain our own health as we cared for and juggled his mother and my parents' issues. Stress was taking its toll. We were having our own physical problems.

Time Off / Finding "Sitters"

Someone else must occasionally "sit" with a loved one. Every human being, caregivers included, need a few hours away: to do something enjoyable, to shop, to see a personal physician, to get a haircut, or go to a movie. There is, at best, a tedium to the provider of 24/7 care. Over time, elevated levels of stress...physical, mental, emotional, can be expected.

During the six years of caregiving, Stan and I used approximately 14 different sitters on a very limited basis. Usually we hired for two hours at a time. Most sitters came only once. Two were promising, but they became pregnant and were no longer available. A neighbor stayed with Olivia two or three times during the day so Stan could do repairs on our house. There was no other suitable family support. Stan's daughter lived out of state, as did a niece and nephew.

The average babysitter hasn't the knowledge or skills to watch over a dementia patient. Olivia needed a professional caregiver or nurse, or someone who had been intimately involved with a family member living with the disease. Any of these would be prepared for the constantly changing abilities and potentially catastrophic reactions.

There were only three people Stan and I felt totally comfortable with as care providers: my mother, the church lady, and one friend.

In the early years of caregiving, my mother was able to take in Olivia, allowing Stan and I to go out, by ourselves, for a special occasion, maybe our anniversary or a birthday. Our break was limited to three hours and took a lot of pre-planning! As Olivia and my Dad's conditions worsened, going out became a rarity or impossible.

Several times, Stan and I paid the church lady to stay with Olivia overnight. We put his mother to bed. Then we had a few hours to relax and sleep in our <u>own house</u> without much worry. We were right next door.

This same church lady stayed with Olivia, allowing us to go on a 3-4 day vacation to the beach at least twice over the years. Additionally, she would take Olivia to a special church service for healing every couple of months, or to her house for a few hours giving Stan a short break. She was a life saver. Stan and I were very grateful.

Another friend, who had cared for her own father-in-law when he suffered from dementia, sat with Olivia several times. When she adopted her three grandchildren and began working for a care facility, her availability to us ended.

I discovered a church in town that had a memory-impaired day care for a charge of $60/day, which included lunch and a snack. Stan was unsure how his mother would react to strangers and to confinement in a "lock-down" area. Olivia was accustomed to a degree of freedom. I observed for a short while at this day care, but saw only two attendees participating in any activity. Only these two might have befriended Olivia. Stan never brought his mother there but it could have worked in an emergency, had we needed it.

Housebound

Ultimately, my husband and I stopped trying to get away together entirely. It was too complicated to find trustworthy sitters, too expensive to pay them, or too onerous to prepare Olivia for a "drop-off". Just to see a movie cost us $80 for 4 hours, including commute time into town…$80.00 for a movie and a sitter!

Typically, one of us ran errands; the other remained at home to sit with Olivia. We rarely had time to be alone together as a couple.

Loss of Vision, Hearing, Reading and Writing Skills

Olivia complained to Stan and me that she couldn't hear or see. One time, insisting she couldn't hear us, we repeated ourselves, louder and louder, until we were yelling right next to her ear. Her hearing aids tested fine, but if we asked her a question, she often responded with something entirely different. We finally realized that when she said she couldn't "hear", it really meant she <u>didn't understand</u> what we were saying.

Stan took his mother to the eye doctor. She tested 20/20 vision. That confirmed to us that she could "see", but <u>not comprehend</u> what she saw. The Alzheimer's group leader also explained that older people develop tunnel vision. This is even more pronounced in a patient with dementia, only having a small line of sight directly forward.

Olivia often told visitors that she was reading lots of books, but if asked any question about what book it was, the author or content, she wasn't able to describe anything. "Reading" simply meant she had a book open in her lap and was turning the pages or looking at a picture. It was a way of passing time during the day as she sat in her chair.

Stan and I suggested Olivia write thank you notes to people who had been kind to her, or respond back to a letter she had received. She would write part of a sentence, repeating the same words over and over on the page and never complete a full thought. Her notes weren't mailed. Olivia quickly lost coordination, comprehension, reading and writing skills.

Interesting Dress

In the past, my mother-in-law had dressed impeccably for work and church. She had a closet full of nice clothes including dresses, work suits and blazers that now were never worn. She could still wear most of the dress blouses, but I weeded out a good portion of the remainder.

Now, Olivia's dressing choices were quite interesting. We continued to let her dress herself, but in the winter she claimed herself ready to go out, but had no socks, nor shoes, nor jacket. In the summer, she would come out of her bedroom with sweat pants topped by her nightgown, topped by two different shirts, a hat, sunglasses, and a heavy winter scarf held on with a clothes pin. It was hard not to laugh. She looked like a homeless person wearing every piece of clothing they owned. If we were going anywhere, Stan and I would remind his mother of the season, its appropriate attire; then help with any re-dressing required.

Decorations and Stuffed Toys

I love every holiday and always decorated our home for each season. Olivia especially liked the scarecrow and the stuffed witch I put out for Halloween. We had Easter eggs at Easter, pilgrims at Thanksgiving and special ornaments on the tree at Christmas with Olivia's name on them. My mother-in-law enjoyed having a soft stuffed doll and a stuffed dog on her bed. She liked holding these. It took some getting used to witnessing an 86 year old woman with toys, and relating to her, now with the mind of a two or three year old.

We Learn As We Go

There was no way to teach Olivia anything new or "bring her back" to reality because she simply could not remember. Instead, Stan and I had to adjust **our** way of thinking and behaving. **We** had to learn how to adapt to each new situation as it evolved.

My mother and I constantly compared notes about what my father was doing and what my mother-in-law was doing. A lot of their symptoms were the same, although some things were totally different. My mother and I were a great support for each other in our caregiving experiences. Most of all, our faith in God, and prayer, helped us get through the most difficult and challenging times.

Emotional Support

Stan was especially isolated from everyone and everything. He was with his mother all day long. He would have a short break after I got home from work and took over. On the weekends, he could disappear into our house and putter in his workshop or visit a friend nearby as an escape from the stress.

My emotional support came from talks with my mother, my co-workers and other friends, including the church people. At least I got to leave for work, see other people and have normal conversations.

I'm sure my co-workers got tired of hearing my daily chronicles. Even though they may not have had the experience of dementia in their family to offer suggestions, just having them listen to me was an enormous help. Many times I was anxious to leave work, but didn't want to go home to deal with the situation there.

Hoarding

The walls in Olivia's bedroom became covered with pictures and magazine articles she taped or pinned up. She dug things she wanted to salvage out of the garbage can and brought them into her room. She picked up rocks from outside, collected seashells, and anything else she could hold and bring in. Eventually, I had to go into her room while she was eating dinner, so I could clear out some of the clutter. She never mentioned that she realized her prized "collection" was gradually disappearing.

Laundry, Clothes and Dressing Issues

Olivia had continued to do her own laundry for quite some time, but now she didn't remember which buttons to push on the washing machine. She asked how to get the water in and forgot that detergent was needed. If Stan or I asked her to sort or fold her laundry, she would lay down flat on her bed, pick up an item and put it back down. The clean clothes were now left in a heap on her bed or in the clothes bin. She had lost all sense of routine and daily living activities.

Olivia ironed her clothes for a time. Stan and I were concerned that the ironing board would collapse or that his mother would burn herself on the iron. We took them away.

It was becoming overwhelming for Olivia to manipulate buttons and zippers and too hard for Stan or I to help her get dressed. To make our life easier, I bought Olivia permanent press clothes: simple pants with stretch waistbands, pullover tops, and pullover nightgowns instead of pajamas. The new clothes were "presents" for Olivia and made her feel special and that she had been rewarded.

Things in Disarray / The Messy Phase

Olivia began to change clothes several times during the day. Every time she came out of her room she had on a different outfit. At first I thought it was because she could still change clothes herself, but it was probably part of the repetitive activity symptom of the disease and the need to keep hands busy.

In addition, Stan and I realized that every time his mother woke up from a nap, she was disoriented. She thought it was the beginning of a new day and she had to put clean clothes on. She would wish us a "good morning" whether it was noon, afternoon or early evening.

To help Olivia continue to dress herself, I put labels on her dresser drawers so she could find pants, tops and socks easily. But by this time in her disease, she no longer understood what these words were. Now, she took everything out of the drawers and threw the clothes all over the bed and floor. Olivia could no longer make a decision about what to wear, what each article of clothing was, or what to do with it.

I didn't know which clothes on the floor were clean or dirty and was constantly picking up. Olivia's room was a disaster. Stan and I finally convinced his mother to let us handle her laundry. Going forward, we picked out and handed her one piece of clothing at a time to put on. When she undressed, I immediately put those clothes in the laundry.

Olivia also became sloppy at the table, dropping food in her lap, on the chair and floor, so I was constantly cleaning there too. She was losing coordination with utensils and couldn't handle a knife and fork at the same time. Messy hands left fingerprints on cabinets and doors. I felt like I was chasing after, cleaning and picking up after a one year old.

The Naked Phase

The next phase in Olivia's decline was the removal of clothes and nakedness. Often, Stan and I would find his mother sitting completely nude in her chair, in the bed or on the floor. We never understood why she did this and she couldn't tell us. We guessed maybe clothes now felt foreign on her or were irritating. Some books indicated it was a matter of fidgeting and keeping occupied.

My husband was not particularly bothered by his mother's nudity and I guess I became accustomed to seeing her that way after awhile. But we always tried to get her clothes back on – especially when she would begin to disrobe at the dinner table and we were trying to eat!

At one bedtime, I tried to get Olivia to change into a nightgown. I was already exhausted and needed sleep. She refused to cooperate, so I yanked off her top and pants and pulled the nightgown over her head. Ten minutes later, I went into her room. She had stripped off the nightgown and was naked. She had thrown the nightgown on the floor. I again pulled it over her head so she wouldn't get cold. This time she gave up the struggle and finally went to sleep.

Long Term Memory Loss

Olivia was now 13 years into her disease. Occasionally, she would ask where her parents were. She didn't remember they had died many years ago. She would ask about her brothers and sister who had also been deceased for a number of years. When another sister died, Olivia vaguely remembered for a week after we told her, and then totally forgot. She was taking anti-depression medication so was not depressed, but continued to be frustrated for not being able to remember.

For some time, my mother-in-law asked about her other children and about one niece. Later, all memories of them were gone and she asked about no one. There was a time when Olivia looked totally confused. Stan asked if she knew who he was. She just answered "boy". "Boy" now meant "son". However, she always remembered her own name.

Further Decline and Congestive Heart Failure

My mother-in-law declined over the last six months of her life. Congestive heart failure caused swelling in the feet, legs, stomach and face, making her almost unrecognizable at times. It looked as if she were pregnant. She couldn't get any pants over her belly, so I had to buy bigger, looser clothes for her to wear.

Olivia was put on a diuretic (Lasix) which she took twice a day. The diuretic caused her to have accidents which were understandable. She also had to wear support hose which were uncomfortable and hard to manage taking on and off during all the toileting problems.

Olivia also developed open, oozing sores on her legs from the lack of circulation. She continually picked at them. Stan and I had to follow a specific wound treatment procedure. Often, Olivia pulled off the gauze dressings which were wrapped around her legs. This negated the whole sterilization process and required a lot of re-cleaning and re-wrapping throughout the day. Wearing long pants eventually discouraged his mother from doing this since the gauze bandaging was out of sight. Even with antibiotics, her healed sores were replaced by new ones.

Olivia seemed to get stuck in a rut and ask the same question over and over repeatedly for hours until it would drive Stan and me crazy. Every minute was new to her, as she couldn't remember the past or what she had just asked. Even though we would try to re-direct the conversation to something else, his mother continually came back to her previous thought like a broken record. There were times when I walked in the door from work, Stan ran right past me and out of the house just to get away from it all.

Advanced Mobility Issues

Phase 3 (advanced dementia) *– this stage can last from 1-2 years. In the final stage of the disease, individuals lose the ability to respond to their environment, to carry on a conversation and, eventually, to control movement. They may still say words or phrases, but communicating pain becomes difficult.*

Now, Olivia's walks on the ramp at home greatly diminished. She would say "it's too hot; it's too cold; I'll do it later…..". Stan and I tried the approach that we were the ones who needed to walk; would she join us? That no longer worked. Stan and I eventually gave up as we were wasting our breath. But we knew if she stopped walking, she would no longer be able to. Then she would be bedridden, no longer able to get up, to do anything, or to go anywhere, anymore. Olivia was only walking from her bedroom into the living room or into the dining room to eat. The less she walked, the more her muscles atrophied and her brain forgot how to walk.

She began to fall more frequently – sometimes every other day, sometimes three times in one day. The doctor said there was really nothing we could do to prevent Olivia from falling. He still wanted her to attempt walking on her own as much as possible. Luckily, there was soft carpeting throughout most of the house, unlike the hard tile floors that were installed in her previous home and had caused injuries. Olivia toddled along fine one minute, on the floor the next. That part of her brain would click on and off suddenly. Major motor skills were being affected.

The Balance Class had taught the participants that if they felt like they were going to fall, to just sit down, so they wouldn't get hurt. So now, Olivia was "sitting down" on the floor a lot. One time she fell into the wall and put a hole in the sheetrock. Other times, if she fell against a dresser or cabinet, the skin would tear off her arm or elbow. She required bandaging. Stan or I were frequently administering first aid.

Olivia must have had very strong bones. It was a miracle she never broke anything other than a slight fracture in her wrist. That fix up did not last. Overnight, Olivia managed to pull out all the gauze stuffing from the cast and wriggle her hand out. Imagine my surprise when she appeared the next morning without the cast. I found it in her garbage can! When I asked Olivia why she removed the cast, she said it "bothered" her. She had no concept that the cast was to help her wrist heal. The doctor said it would be useless to put another cast on. It was just a hairline fracture. Leave it alone.

After one fall, Olivia complained that her back was "broke". I told her that if it was broken she wouldn't be able to stand or walk, but decided she better get x-rays to be sure she was alright. She was fine, other than being bruised.

Stan and I had to interpret what his mother was saying as if she were a toddler trying to explain things to us. She knew something hurt and this was her way of describing that feeling. "Broke" = Hurts. In her lack of understanding, she was also trying to figure out what we were telling her as well. Comprehension and translations had to work both ways. Verbal communication was fading.

Another night, Stan and I heard a crash and found his mother on the bathroom floor. I called 911 and she was taken to the hospital. We wanted to be sure nothing was broken and that she didn't have a concussion. Tests showed she was fine, but the medical emergencies were increasing.

Now there were times when Olivia could not remember how to move her body at all – how to roll over or place one foot in front of the other to walk. Once she fell in the kitchen and lay on the floor for half an hour. Stan and I tried to explain to her how to get up. No success. We didn't want to lift her and hurt ourselves. It was impossible for us to pick up 140 pounds when she couldn't follow instructions to assist by pushing or pulling herself up. Olivia scooted and squirmed like a worm all over the floor. She wiggled on her behind, on her back and her side. Grabbing the chair legs, she got underneath the table, then back out. It was truly a pathetic sight to watch.

Then Olivia wanted us to put her dinner plate on the floor so she could eat! We told her she would have to get up, thinking that would be motivation for her to stand. Stan and I decided that if she couldn't get herself up shortly, we would have to call 911 to come and lift her.

Instead, Stan and I got a protective mattress pad, rolled his mother onto it and then dragged her from the kitchen onto the soft living room rug near a chair. It took Stan's mother another half hour to finally comprehend how to push and stand up. Before, when she had fallen, Olivia had always been able to get herself back up in 10-15 minutes. This time, it was almost an hour until the light switch in her brain clicked on. Her mobility and comprehension were getting much worse.

Going "Home"

Olivia began to say she wanted to go "home". At first Stan and I thought she might be referring to one of her previous houses over the years. However when we asked her about them, it was never the right place. We would tell her this was the only house she had anymore.

Olivia was now lost in her surroundings and searching for the safety and security that a familiar home brings. In addition, Stan and I decided that his mother was talking about going home to the comfort of God and God's kingdom. She was coming to terms with dying and leaving this world.

Olivia also began to ask us if she could sleep here for the night. Then she'd ask "Where should I go? Where's the bedroom? Where's the bathroom?" Stan or I would either have to go with her or tell her "go straight, turn left, turn right". Nothing was familiar to her anymore.

Another Hospital Stay and Medicare Home Health

Olivia had another hospital stay to treat her fluid retention, a urinary tract infection (UTI-which made her even more confused and combative), and the open sores caused by her congestive heart failure. She fell in the hospital, hitting her head. They put sensors on her bed and on the floor in case she got up again unassisted. Back home, there were many times when she had a totally "gone" look and blank stare. You could tell just by looking at her what state of mind she was in and what would be in store for us that day.

Olivia's doctor ordered Home Health care, the cost of which was covered by Medicare. A caregiver gave Olivia a shower twice a week, a nurse came twice a week to take Olivia's vitals, and a physical therapist came twice a week to work on strengthening her muscles and her walking. However, as with the Balance Class, Olivia thought physical therapy was a social visit instead of a work out for her physical well being. She just wanted to sit and talk. Soon, physical therapy was discontinued.

Olivia loved being the center of attention with all the home health caregivers fussing around her. She always had a very sweet disposition with them and any other visitors.

Even as Olivia lost many physical abilities, her social skills remained active for quite some time. Often when other people saw her, they didn't realize there was anything wrong. She looked well and could speak, but had an impaired brain. Conversations were usually limited to a few pleasantries. It was not unless you lived with her, or saw her round the clock for several days at a time, that you were aware of all the serious limitations.

The home health personnel did not come on a set schedule, although they did call a half hour before they came to be sure we were home. Sometimes, all three aids would arrive on the same day, so there was a constant stream of people in and out of the house. Then, no one would come for a few days. Their short visits did not allow enough time for Stan or me to run errands or go to appointments of our own. Since we lived in the country, it took us longer to get anywhere. That was a disadvantage.

Olivia had a habit of chewing on ice cubes. One day she broke part of a tooth implant. Her dentist recommended a specialist who wanted to perform dental surgery. This surgeon was afraid that if the tooth wasn't fixed, Olivia might develop an infection which could go into her bloodstream. When Stan and I asked Olivia's regular doctor about proceeding with the surgery, he said that a patient with dementia should "<u>never have any kind of surgery performed</u>" unless it was for a <u>life threatening</u> condition. We abided by his recommendation.

The dementia patient cannot deal well with most medications and would not understand what is happening. Surgery would be extremely upsetting and stressful to everyone, including us, with the after-care.

Difficulty Sitting and Standing/Needing Proper Furniture

How to sit properly was forgotten. Olivia was plopping down with her full weight. She wound up breaking the webbing in the lawn chairs on the porch. The chairs had to be removed so she wouldn't get hurt.

Olivia's mattress was quite old. Stan and I bought a new one for her thinking it would be more comfortable. We found that the new mattress was a lot higher than the old one and Olivia had trouble getting in and out of bed. If she fell, it would be further to the floor and pose a greater risk of injury. We put the old mattress back on her bed.

The recliners and chairs were all too low and too deep. Others rocked, making it difficult for Olivia to get out of, as it would be for most elderly people. Olivia couldn't sit up straight for very long and would gradually slide down in the living room chair. Sometimes she reclined flat and slid right out of the chair and onto the floor.

Stan and I couldn't afford a lot of new furniture. Instead, I purchased 5" foam cushions to add under the seats and backs of the chairs my mother-in-law sat in. This raised her high enough to make sitting more comfortable and standing up easier. The dining room captain's chairs were good. They had arms to help her push up.

Even though the raised foam cushions helped for awhile, during the last six months of her life, Stan and I had to continually coach his mother. "Stand up" we said. "Lean forward, bend at the waist, hold the walker, push with your legs". More lessons were needed to transfer from the wheelchair to the chair at the dining table. A lot of times, Stan just gave up and pushed his mother in the wheelchair. Even when she did get up, she moved so slowly and we were on a timetable to get things done.

Incontinence and Contamination in the House

Olivia became incontinent and was urinating on the furniture and in her bed: even with two Depends and pads inside those, plus mattress protectors. Stan and I were faced with cleanup of the messes and constant laundry. After an incident on one of the living room recliners, I tried to protect it with a garbage bag and keep Olivia sitting in that chair only so the others wouldn't be ruined.

Typically, when asked if she had to go to the bathroom, Olivia would say "no" – then begin wetting down her leg into her shoes and onto the floor. Luckily, she did not have bowel incontinence or impaction: Stan and I were able to keep her regular by providing over-the-counter Miralax every other day in her coffee.

Stan and I tried to give his mother privacy in the bathroom, but now she was forgetting to put on a new Depends when she was through. We had to check her after she was done. Stan felt uncomfortable doing this, but it did prevent some cleanups.

A few times, we caught Olivia playing in the toilet. She smeared feces on the toilet base and floor, much to our dismay. Once, the three of us were supposed to go to my parents to celebrate my father's birthday. Instead, Stan had to stay to clean up the bathroom and his mother. I went to my parents' house alone. Olivia frequently stripped off her Depends. Sometimes it seemed like she was doing this on purpose to spite us, but I'm sure it was a symptom of her dementia, just as removing the rest of her clothes.

Now Stan and I had to keep checking on his mother in the bathroom, keeping a mop and bucket with Lysol handy at all times. It was at this point, an acquaintance of ours put her demented mother in a nursing home. She couldn't deal with her mother smearing feces on the walls.

Olivia's skin was paper thin. Any fall caused a tear and bleeding on the rugs, bedding, furniture and her clothes. She ripped off her band aids causing additional bleeding. Olivia had been diagnosed with hepatitis C and cirrhosis of the liver (non-typical) from what we assumed were contaminated needles during the time she required insulin shots for her diabetes. As a result, Stan and I had to wear rubber gloves to avoid direct contact with her blood if we had any cuts. I really felt like the manufactured home was contaminated and hated to touch anything. At this point, I was very glad that Stan and I were not caring for Olivia in our own house.

Belligerent

One time Olivia shouted at Stan and me "Get out; go to hell"; "leave me alone"! I felt I was living through "The Invasion of the Body Snatchers". It seemed like the parent we had known and loved for so long was gone and a stranger inhabiting her body.

Putting myself in Olivia's position, I would not want someone following me around and watching me in the bathroom as I did my business. Stan and I told her that for her safety we could not leave her alone. When she replied that Stan "treated her like shit" that put me over the edge. I was quick to come to his defense and yelled back at her. Afterwards, I felt guilty for my behavior. She didn't know any better and was just reacting to her loss of privacy and independence.

Our dilemma, when Olivia got combative, was that Stan and I couldn't pick her up and put her in a crib or playpen as one might with a disruptive toddler having a tantrum. All we could do was exit the room, separate ourselves, and leave her alone until she calmed down.

Within a few minutes Olivia forgot the whole incident, while I was still shaking for hours from the upset. But **I did feel that Stan and I were now being abused by her.**

Another time, Olivia said she "didn't like it here" and "didn't want to be here" anymore. My initial reaction was that she didn't like her home, she didn't like us and she was very ungrateful for the care we were providing. I told her to get her suitcase and pack - Stan and I would take her to the nursing home the next morning. Of course that never happened.

I quickly realized her true meaning was not a personal attack against us. It had nothing to do with us. It had to do with her and her feelings. She didn't like the circumstances she now found herself in. She didn't like being confused, helpless and dependent on others. She wanted her life and her mind back to the way it used to be. Maybe she didn't want to be alive anymore. It was important to keep asking: what is the true meaning behind her words? Again – the interpretation issues.

Stan's mother was occasionally like Dr. Jekyll and Mr. Hyde. One minute she absolutely loved us, the next minute it seemed she hated us. We knew she was lashing out from her frustration, loss of control and the rules we were making that she did not understand. I had to keep reminding myself that the <u>disease</u> was the cause of her actions, but it was hard not to take what she said literally and personally.

To this day I continue to ask for Olivia and God's forgiveness for my snapping back. It was becoming harder for me to remain patient and understanding at all times, especially if I had had a hard day at work and little sleep. But over the 5-1/2 years of care, I only lost my patience with her verbally two or three times.

Working From Home

Caregiving continued to be provided almost entirely by Stan and me. Luckily, the company I worked for had suggested that employees work from home if they were able. I had remodeling done in our house to create a true office for me and I began working from home.

Within two months, I only needed to go into our corporate office twice a week. This was a tremendous benefit to me. Now I could save almost two hours of commuting each day. In addition, I saved gas, the cost of fancier work clothes and eating out. I no longer had to race to run errands at the end of an already stressful work day, race to get home, and race to prepare dinner. Working from home relieved a lot of stress and allowed me some time to myself.

Baby Proofing

Olivia was now at the stage when she might potentially swallow something or hurt herself because she didn't know what the item was, or forgot what it was used for. A friend of mine told me that her father-in-law with dementia put everything in his mouth like a baby. I was fearful that Olivia would do this too. One day, I noticed Olivia's face was very red. Stan and I didn't know what she might have put on it, so I removed all lotions, perfumes and deodorant from her room. We never figured out what the irritant was but all potential suspects were now eliminated. Maybe her skin was just becoming more sensitive.

On the Wait List

It was becoming more difficult to care for Olivia, draining both Stan and me. We decided to put his mother on a wait list for a "memory" wing at a care facility. Of course, we both wavered; what was best to do? It was a very hard decision to make and one that brought great guilt to Stan. As difficult as handling his mother had become, I couldn't imagine having to place my own father anywhere. I sympathized with my husband. Would it really be any easier to go to this facility daily after work, 35 miles from our home, to see how his mother was doing?

The potential care facility had primarily shared suites. Although there were separate bedrooms, both patients had to share a bath. I thought this would be a problem because Olivia spent so much time in the bathroom that the other patient would never be able to use it. We might have to move Olivia to a private room which would cost considerably more money. We would cross that road if it happened. The facility had a beauty parlor on site, washed the patient's laundry, had planned activities, and provided transportation to and from doctor's visits.

After two months, the facility called and said they had an opening. We needed to give them a decision by the next morning. Olivia had had an unusually good day. This gave Stan and I hope that we could continue caring for her at home. I told the facility to put my mother-in-law back at the bottom of the wait list. I believe that by Olivia having a really good day at that precise moment, God wanted Olivia to remain with us, because the very next day she was right back to being quite a challenge.

We Go Away

Stan and I went out of state for four days to attend my son's wedding. We left Olivia in the care of the church lady who came and stayed with her in the manufactured home. We could have left Olivia at a memory impaired facility for respite care, but the church lady was available and Olivia was familiar with her and loved her.

Unfortunately, while Stan and I were gone, Olivia fell twice on the second night. When we returned, the church lady said she could no longer handle the responsibility of Olivia's care, especially the wound care. She was also afraid of a liability issue. Stan and I fully understood her concerns and position. This was overwhelming for anyone, but now we were totally without any trusted care relief.

Returning home, the caregiving seemed so much worse to me. After several days to ourselves, with freedom and good times at the joyous wedding celebration, we were again smacked in the face with my mother-in-law's increasingly critical condition. Stan and I decided that when the care facility called next, we would place his mother there whether she was having a good day or not.

Stan began saying his mother smelled, even immediately after she had a shower. I did not notice the smell, but he thought it was the "smell of death".

Often at the dinner table, when Stan and I were conversing, Olivia would just start talking and not make sense. She did not comprehend that we were speaking or understand what we were saying, but she was still trying to join in.

Olivia spent most days sitting in her chair in the living room, dozing. If Olivia was awake, she could still observe what I was doing in the kitchen or around the house. Now, even when the church people came, she often slept through the visit. The progression of her dementia and the congestive heart failure was too taxing on her brain to remain alert and involved in surroundings.

Sudden Cessation of Walking and Eating

One day, about two months later, Olivia suddenly could not stand after lunch. At dinner, she didn't eat. It was all Stan and I could do to lift her into the wheelchair and then from the wheelchair into her bed that night. I left a message with the doctor that a hospital bed was now required. All night, Olivia called "help – I can't get up". There was nothing we could do for her. It appeared she would now be bedridden.

In the morning, I called the Medicare home health nurse. She wanted Stan and me to take Olivia to the doctor. I explained that we couldn't lift her to get her there. The nurse told us to take Olivia to the hospital instead, so Stan called 911. Once at the hospital, Olivia became extremely combative and ripped out the IV placed in her arm. She was admitted and sedated. Still, Stan and I expected his mother to improve again. She had improved numerous times in the past.

The End

We visited Olivia in the hospital the next day. She seemed to be asleep. Stan and I thought that was due to the sedation, although I noticed the words "comfort care" written on the board in her room. The doctor wasn't there. When asked, the head nurse didn't inform us of any issues or great concerns. At 11:30 that night, a nurse called us to the hospital. Olivia's breathing had changed. She died before we could arrive. Congestive heart failure had taken her life before the dementia, which she had battled for 15 years.

My husband took his mother's death very hard. Being with her every day and night for 5-1/2 years, he had become very close to her. Her whole life and survival had depended on us. I felt good knowing that she lived 5-1/2 years longer than she would have, had we not intervened. We did the very best we could to make her life, during that time, as pleasant as possible. I know she had many enjoyable moments and that deep down she appreciated our care.

Stan and I again moved our clothes and personal items, this time back into our own house. I continued to feel Olivia's energy and presence in the manufactured home as I began extensive cleaning and sorting of her possessions.

Now the process of obtaining an EIN and Stan becoming the Personal Representative of the Estate began. These legal aspects and Probate dragged on another year due to the family issues. Eventually, the manufactured home was sold and the proceeds divided according to Olivia's Will. Several months later, Jason hung himself.

While Stan and I both grieved for his mother, I was immediately and totally immersed in the care of my father. He was still alive and in the final stage of his Alzheimer's disease. His care story follows.

MY FAMILY

My Dad was a joy-filled, intelligent, hardworking man. He always put family first; how he loved us and our extended family! Growing up, he left our screen doors open and welcoming to all. He never spoke unkindly of anyone and was always thinking of others and how he could help them. He was truly a remarkable man - a mentor to many; encouraging both young and old; loved and respected by all.

He remained, always, physically fit and mentally active and had such a well-rounded, full life. He excelled in his work and had high morale ethics. Dad embraced boating, swimming, camping, hiking, poetry and play-writing,

gardening, oil painting and home improvement projects. We shared a common love of the outdoors, flowers, music, museums and canoeing. Dad enjoyed being on or near the water, was very active in church, singing in choir and traveling. He was always ready for an adventure. He and Mom took trips each summer in the U.S., Canada and Europe. They also went on several cruises.

After Dad retired at age 63, my parents purchased a summer home on a lake in Maine. There, Dad could sail and enjoy a quiet life in the North woods. I, my son and my husband, also enjoyed numerous vacations spent with them there.

The Beginning of Health Issues

About ten years later, Mom started having trouble with arthritis. She could no longer sit in the car for the 13 hour drive from their permanent house to the summer home in Maine. Dad had several TIA's (mini-strokes which could destroy areas of the brain). He was treated for high cholesterol and required a heart monitor. The closest major hospital and specialist for treatment was in Portland, four hours away. Both parents really needed to be close to doctors and not live in such a remote location. Reluctantly, they sold the summer home and purchased a house near the Gulf Coast, several hours from me.

Over the next decade, Mom battled cancer, walking problems and an infection which lasted for months, keeping her confined to the house. She also had pain from her increasingly severe osteoarthritis. She went to a chiropractor, tried acupuncture treatments and various medications. Her condition now required the use of a walker and a motorized chair. Also, she had diabetes.

While Dad was caring for Mom, he told no one of pains in his chest. These he had been having for quite a while. When Mom pressed Dad to get checked, he was rushed for an emergency stent operation to correct a severe blockage in his aeorta.

Not long after his surgery, with multiple health issues, Mom and Dad decided to move into a retirement community closer to me. A year or two later, Dad began exhibiting signs of short term memory loss.

Loss of Memory and Abilities

Stage 1 (mild dementia) *– This stage can last from 2-4 years. In the early stages of Alzheimer's, a person may function independently. He or she may <u>still drive, work and be part of social activities</u>. Despite this, the person may feel as if he or she is having memory lapses, such as <u>forgetting familiar words or the location of everyday objects</u>. Friends, family or neighbors begin to notice difficulties. During a detailed medical interview, doctors may be able to detect problems in memory or concentration. Common difficulties include<u>: problems describing the right word or name; trouble remembering names when introduced to new people; difficulty performing tasks in social or work settings</u>; forgetting material just read; losing or misplacing a valuable object; increasing <u>difficulty planning or organizing</u>.*

In 2006, after dealing with my in-laws' dementia issues for five years, my father, who was now 87 years old, began to show dementia symptoms. There was no previous family history of dementia that I was aware of. At least I had a better idea about what to expect with my father, but **now there were three parents with this disability at the same time!**

Dad had had previous cataract surgeries in both eyes, but one eye was unsuccessful. He complained of double vision. Now, he was having trouble reading. Dad's eyes were checked again. He did have some issues, but it went beyond that. He could see and identify letters, but couldn't piece the letters together into words. While leading chapel services at the retirement community where my parents now lived, Dad was having difficulty following the scriptures and order of the service. He also couldn't seem to remember people or their names. Mom was very worried about him.

She realized Dad was having memory issues. She knew they both needed more help, so once again, they moved closer to me. I spent two months accompanying my parents to look at houses. They purchased a single story home, which was suitable to my mother's handicap, and just 20 minutes from me. It was also on my route to and from work, so it would be an easy stop when they needed assistance.

After my parents' house closing, Stan and I helped them settle in. Dad was frustrated trying to unpack. He kept losing things. He was upset and crying because he was unable to connect any of the electronic equipment. Stan and I did that for him. Dad couldn't even remember which buttons to push to turn the stereo on and off. We put red tape on the buttons to help him. He seemed to become forgetful more frequently and had lapses in memory, including the ability to do things which previously had been no trouble for him.

As a couple, Stan and I spent time helping my parents while we were on a brief respite from my in-laws' issues. Stan remodeled my parents' house: making a walk-in shower for my mother, changing some flooring, and widening the doorways to accommodate the width of Mom's motorized chair.

No sooner had the remodeling of their house been completed than my mother went into sepsis with a urinary blockage and Stage 3 kidney failure. Luckily, at that time, Dad still knew how to use the phone. He called me on my way to work and said there was something very wrong with Mom.

We rushed her to the hospital, where she was admitted to the intensive care unit. She was near death. Mom suffered from "white coat syndrome". An unpleasant dental visit experienced early in her life, so terrified her that a doctor visit, no matter how routine, caused her enormous anxiety. This hospital stay would be very traumatic for her.

After surgery, Mom refused to speak or open her mouth to eat. The staff tied down her hands for a short time because she was pulling out the IV and not cooperating. She didn't know who we were. We learned from Mom later that she believed everyone was the devil, practicing voodoo, trying to poison her and burn her alive. This was probably the effects of anesthesia, and the burning sensation at the site of her operation.

Mom thought Dad was a POW pilot she had met in Europe during WWII. When she started talking in German, I was called to come and interpret. She said she so loved her husband and daughter (not knowing it was me by her bedside) and that God would protect her. Her discomposed behavior continued for several weeks. I was alarmed and frightened for her. The doctor explained to me that many of the elderly go into this state during hospital stays. Although the blockage had been removed, and Mom was physically doing better, she was not coming out of this mental "fog". The doctor said she might need to be transferred to the psychiatric floor! Losing her mind seemed far worse to me than any physical battle she faced.

Mom finally began to drink some soda, only after confirming the bottle had not been opened to allow anyone to sneak "poison" into it. In an effort to bring her back to us, I played cassettes of my piano and organ recitals. Maybe if she recognized my music, it would confirm who I was.

Miraculously, when Dad and I arrived the next morning, Mom knew who we were and started speaking coherently in English. It was Mother's Day and I thanked God for giving my mother back to me. What a blessing!

Her hospital stay was followed by three months in rehab, recovering from bed sores, a broken hip sustained entering the hospital, and learning to walk again.

Dad and I visited Mom in rehab daily. During that time, I ran errands, made sure Dad had food in the house, and was eating. He wound up with a severe case of the shingles on his face very near his eyes. I'm sure it was a result of the stress of Mom being away. Happily, with medication he recovered. Once Mom returned home, things stabilized for a short time.

I organized a surprise party for my parents in celebration of their 60th wedding anniversary and my mothers return to better health. Eight of their friends from around the country came for a long weekend to join the festivities. Everyone had a wonderful time. Little did we know then, but it would be the last time all of them would get together. Three months later, Mom had a second hospitalization for the removal of her gallbladder, hernia and intestine repair.

The first two years my parents lived near me, Dad continued to work outdoors, trimming bushes, mowing the grass and tending flowers. That decreased in time. Even with a battery-operated lawnmower (which eliminated exertion from a pull cord), summer remained hot. Also, Dad could lose balance on the sloped lawn. My parents hired yard care services.

Helping my parents was different than assisting my in-laws. My mother had her mental faculties and there were no legal dilemmas to face. My parents Wills, Durable POA's and medical POA's were up to date and they had me named as backup. I carried those documents, as well as both of their medical histories, medications and list of doctors, with me at all times.

Stage 2 (moderate dementia) - *This stage may last from 2-10 years. The person can <u>no longer perform routine tasks, has lost their short term memory, lost the ability to know day and time, becomes lost or loses things, doesn't understand relationships, needs to be accompanied everywhere, becomes very suspicious and may have hallucinations.</u> Moderate Alzheimer's is typically the longest stage. As the disease progresses, there will be word confusion, frustration, anger and unexpected behavior – such as <u>refusal to bathe</u>. Damage to nerve cells in the brain can make it difficult to express thoughts and perform routine tasks. At this point, symptoms will be noticeable to others. They include: <u>forgetfulness of recent and past events, personal history, moodiness or withdrawal especially in socially or mentally challenging situations, inability to recall address or telephone number,</u> high school or college experiences, <u>confusion about immediate location, date or time of day. Expect that help will be needed to choose proper clothing</u> for the season or occasion. Expect there may be trouble controlling bladder and bowels. Anticipate changes in sleep patterns (daytime <u>sleeping, nighttime restlessness); increased risk of wandering</u> and becoming lost. There will be <u>personality and behavioral changes</u>, including suspiciousness, <u>delusions and compulsive repetitive actions,</u> such as hand-wringing or tissue shredding.*

Dad had always loved flowers. Now, when my mother bought some plants for him, he could not get the dirt or plants into pots. Gardening became another job for Mom to do.

Painting had always been a love of Dads. He was very talented in painting scenery, the ocean and water. Now he could barely put his ideas to the canvas and was upset with his lack of ability. Finally, he gave up all attempts at painting which was really a shame. Suggesting Dad color with crayons or finger paint seemed too demeaning. Programs are springing up around the country where dementia patients can express themselves through painting. These are probably most successful in early dementia. Olivia and Dad were both past that stage.

Dad could also no longer do the daily crossword puzzles that he and Mom had previously been able to solve together. He willingly gave up driving because he became confused in the neighborhood and forgot how to get home. He no longer knew left from right and things didn't look familiar. Since Mom could drive everywhere he accepted that. He still wanted to keep his keys, even though he couldn't identify one key from another. Actually, this was good because it eliminated a lot of risk.

Mom put red tape on the house key so Dad could locate it easily. That way he could help her into the house after shopping.

Dad also insisted on keeping his wallet. It was something he knew he should always have and he didn't want it taken away. Now, it contained only his identification, his list of medications, doctors, a few dollar bills – "in case he had to pay for something". It allowed him to maintain that dignity.

Dad could no longer do simple arithmetic. This was very shocking since he had been a cost accountant for a major Fortune 500 company during his career. At home, Mom had always handled paying the bills and banking, so that was not an issue, but Dad was upset that he could no longer manage his stocks and investments.

A good portion of Dad's abilities had disappeared. It was hard to see the decline from his previously vibrant life. At this point, Dad could still manage his personal care.

Vacations

After my father-in-law passed away, Stan and I took my mother-in-law and my parents on vacation with us. They had to be accompanied everywhere due to their dementia and handicaps. On the first trip, we stayed in two cabins at the State Park. My mother was with my father in one cabin and my mother-in-law stayed with Stan and me in the other. Everyone had a good time. Dad especially, loved being able to see the water again. We even went on a paddle wheel lunch cruise which happened to coincide on my parents' Anniversary.

The next summer, on the second trip with all of our parents, both my father and mother-in-law's dementia were considerably worse. Even though we were all together in one large rental house on the lake, Dad and Olivia were disoriented and confused, being in a strange place. Dad couldn't find his way from one room to another. In addition, we had to drag so many things with us for the parents' care that the trip wound up being very taxing on all. That was the last adventure going away from home with them.

Medication is Started

Within the year, Dad was having major memory trouble. His doctor started him on Aricept for the dementia. Later, the drug Namenda was added to help Dad perform daily activities.

The cost of these drugs was very high. The usual cost for Aricept 10 mg was $1,100 for a 90 day supply, versus $225 through a drug plan. The cost for Namenda 20 mg was $1,120 for 90 days compared to $180 on a drug plan. After the first few months, Mom enrolled Dad in a prescription program. In doing this, my parents saved thousands of dollars on these two medications.

How Can We Take Care of Them All?

Due to the overlapping care needs of my mother-in-law and my parents, I really thought Stan was going to have to stay with his mother and I was going to have to move in with my parents. It was difficult running back and forth from one house to the other.

The second option was to have everyone under one roof. I really didn't think that would work. The third option was to move my parents into our house with me, with Stan in the manufactured home, next door, with his mother. Then we could at least get everyone together, see each other at dinner. It would be like a full-fledged nursing compound. For the moment, Stan and I maintained care as it was, but kept all these options open.

Depression

Dad acknowledged his disease, unlike my mother-in-law. He was aware of its progression and that he was getting worse. Often, when I stopped by, both parents were crying together. They knew the future did not look promising and they had lost hope. There was no cure for Alzheimer's. Being diagnosed with Alzheimer's was a slow death sentence. My parents' friends were also having major health issues, entering care facilities, or dying one by one. Depression and loss seemed to be their constant companion now.

Just as someone smiling is contagious, my parents' depressive mood became contagious to me. When I suggested to Mom that both she and Dad start medication, Mom said she wasn't depressed and they didn't need to take more prescriptions. Had they been on medication, I think they would have had a much easier time coping with Dad's disease, but that decision was Mom's.

Daily Life

For a while, we could still go out as a family, taking a ride in the car, going out to eat, or enjoying a game of Skip-Bo or Rummy Kubes at home. Later, games became too confusing for Dad. He could not remember the rules and said he could not see the cards, even with large print, or count the dots on the dominoes. He shied away from the challenge and became reluctant to play because he realized he couldn't actively participate anymore. We suggested he become Mom's "coach". In doing so, he still had the successful outcome of a "team" win.

Now, when the family went out to eat, neither Dad nor Olivia could make sense of the menu. Someone else had to order for them. We always went at an off-hour and requested seating in a quiet, back corner of the restaurant to avoid noise and distractions which would make them anxious and upset.

Outings for Mom and Dad were now limited to the food store two miles away, to church three miles away, and to doctors' visits. We no longer had holiday celebrations at my house because Dad didn't know where he was and wanted to go back to the security of his home after an hour.

Dad still liked to get dressed up for church and look nice. Mom and I bought Dad new clothes in colors that complimented him. We told Dad how dapper he looked.

When Mom disposed of Dad's old clothes, he took them out of the garbage and put them back in his closet.

Mom of course, had to go food shopping. Previously, she had relied on Dad to get items off the shelves that she couldn't reach from her motorized chair. Now, when they arrived at the store, Dad became upset and agitated, wanting to go home. Mom would only be able to pick up one or two items and then have to leave. Dad was afraid of being around people, activity and commotion. It was a world that had now become a strange and confusing place to him.

Luckily, my parents' grocery store accepted call-in orders. An employee would collect the items on their list and Mom would drive there to pick up and pay for the order. Even so, Mom had to get Dad in the car for the drive over, into the store, out and drive home.

Dad had begun taking his seatbelt off and trying to open the van door while Mom drove. An obvious safety concern! Now, for them to go anywhere, a third person was indispensable in the vehicle to watch Dad. Otherwise, Mom had to wait until I finished work and could go shopping for her. If she needed something right away, she would try to get the neighbor to run pick-up.

Two of my cousins and their spouses from out of state visited us that year. It was so nice to reconnect with family. I wasn't positive if Dad followed the conversations, but we were so happy to see them. Their visit meant a lot to all of us.

He Escapes

About five years into the disease, during the dead of winter and freezing cold, Dad got out of the house in the middle of the night. Luckily, Mom was able to convince him to come back inside without having to chase him through the neighborhood! Immediately, I purchased alarms for their front and back doors.

Now, Mom kept at least one hearing aid in at night so she would be able to hear if Dad escaped again. He complained about being <u>locked up and held captive</u>. I downplayed the alarms, claiming security for Mom and Dad. Also, I told him I had an alarm system in my own house for safety.

In the next year, Dad wandered outside in the wee hours twice, but was coaxed back in by Mom. Sometimes, during the day, he would go out and start dragging patio furniture around the yard. When Mom asked what he was doing he said someone had come to visit and needed a chair. He was hallucinating.

Further Decline/He Doesn't Know Us

<u>Stage 3 (advanced dementia</u>) - This stage can last from 1-2 years. In the final stage of the disease, individuals lose the ability to respond to their environment, to carry on a conversation and, eventually, to control movement. They may still say words or phrases, but communicating pain becomes difficult. As memory and cognitive skills continue to worsen, personality changes may take place and individuals need extensive help with daily activities. At this stage, individuals require full-time, around-the-clock assistance with daily personal care. They lose awareness of recent experiences as well as surroundings. They experience changes in physical abilities, including the ability to walk, sit, and eventually, swallow. They have increasing difficulty communicating. They become vulnerable to infections, especially pneumonia.

Now Dad rarely knew who we were and did not recognize his house. He kept asking Mom what her name was. Even after she told him, he would look quizzically at her, not believing. Maybe he remembered her as she looked in earlier years.

When I visited some of the memory care facilities, I noticed that photographs of the patients at a much younger age were posted outside their rooms. The staff explained that the patient remembered himself at that time in his life.

I recently came across a suggestion to help dementia patients with recognition issues. It recommended creating a photo lineup of the caretaker and the patient at various ages. One might start with a baby picture, followed by toddler, young adult, then pictures every 10 years or so thereafter. I wish I had read about this earlier. I could have tried it with Dad.

Now Dad was even forgetting his own name. He would ask Mom what it was and she would tell him. Other times Mom would say "you know what your name is". Dad would finally answer and be so proud to recite his first, middle and last name. We praised him for those achievements. Mom continued to quiz Dad on this. She wanted to be sure that if he wandered away and was found, he could at least tell someone his name.

When Mom asked Dad who he thought she was, sometimes he could remember her name, but most of the time she had become "the nice lady that takes care of me". That was the saddest part for Mom. He no longer knew her or their shared memories. Their life together was gone to him.

Because Dad didn't know who he was, or who anyone else was, he assumed that no one knew him either. He kept insisting we call the police to verify his identity and to confirm where he was. Dad would plead with Mom to find his missing home and just let him sleep in his bed. Sometimes, he thought he was in a hotel and we were hotel employees not allowing him to stay in his room, yet also preventing him from leaving the premises.

During one of these episodes, and in order to calm him down, a neighbor called and pretended he was the police. The neighbor tried to assure Dad that he knew who Dad was, that Dad was in his own house, and that no one was going to kick him out. This eventually appeased him.

Another issue Mom faced was sleeping in the same bed with Dad. Since he didn't know who she was any longer, she often slept in the recliner because he said he couldn't share a bed with a strange woman. Other times, he insisted she get into bed because he was her father and she had to do what he told her.

Dad no longer knew me either. Once, I sat with him and could tell he didn't know who I was, but he never asked me my name. He just kept looking at me and frowning. After Mom returned, he asked her who I was and she told him. Dad said he thought I must have been related to him in some way because I "looked a lot like him".

It was upsetting that Dad no longer recognized me, but he commented that I was nice and it was good to be around a smiling, happy person. It made me feel better knowing that he had been content for a little while as we enjoyed listening to some classical music together; but I was very sad that he wasn't having many smiling, happy moments anymore. He had always enjoyed life, been the one joking and creating a playful, enthusiastic, bonding experience and camaraderie. In the past, it was guaranteed that if Dad was present, everyone would be having fun along with him.

It was especially heartbreaking for Mom on her birthdays and their anniversaries when Dad didn't remember having a wife, what that meant, or anything about their wedding. He wasn't able to go out shopping for a gift, or read possible cards to give Mom. I often bought these on his behalf. With great difficulty, he would scratch a mark at the bottom as his signature. By this time he didn't comprehend at all what was going on.

Mom managed to deal with the stress through her strong faith in God. Her link to the world outside of caregiving in their house was via e-mail and phone calls, prayers from friends, people at church and distant family.

Somewhere in the Past

Mom and I started being lectured by Dad about working hard to get a good job, going to college and finding someone nice to marry. He got the two of us confused as people and sometimes spoke as if I were still in high school. Other times, he talked as if he was in the Army.

It was impossible to get Dad to be "in the present". Communication with him had to be in whatever period of time he believed he was in.

Our faces were no longer familiar to Dad. We were not the family he remembered. He forgot who Stan was and that we were married. He couldn't understand why I would leave to go back to my own house. He continued to confuse Mom and me and wondered why she would be leaving him, when it was actually me.

I'm sure Dad felt lost and abandoned when everyone he remembered seemed to be gone. We were all just strangers. He knew my name was something important to remember, but he didn't associate my name with my face.

About this time, I decided to write a "Tribute to Dad", since I knew he wasn't going to remember anything much longer. I wanted to let him know what he had meant to me, to gather pictures from his past that might jog his memory. I presented it on his birthday and he cried when I was through. He was touched by my effort, but I know he no longer recognized any of the people in the pictures. At least I could use this as a memorial when Dad passed away.

Above is the thank you note Dad wrote me after this birthday tribute (a year and a half before his death). His memory had greatly declined and he struggled to write words and communicate his thoughts.

> *"I love you and thank you for your tribute for my my birthday which makes very appreciation of your love of me many thanks for your love of me. You are a wonderful person – for your. Thanks of you and love of me and Mom."* Dad

Dad wrote less and less. Eventually, he had great difficulty scribbling "Dad" at the bottom of my holiday or birthday card. Then he was unable to write anything at all. Over the next year, he gradually lost the ability to follow a conversation, to understand the news or what he saw on television. He was upset and confused by everything around him.

When I was young, I never fully appreciated what a fabulous person and great role model my father had been. Our home was always filled with the love and encouragement of my parents. It was not until I was much older that I realized how lucky I was to be their daughter.

Now when we got together, since Dad and Olivia could no longer comprehend card games or dominoes, we played simple relay games instead. Two competent people and one incapacitated parent were placed on each team. First, a ping pong ball had to be balanced on a plastic spoon while walking across the room. Even though Olivia held the ball with her hand, preventing it from falling off, she managed to walk to the other side.

Next, the ping pong ball had to be pushed across the floor with a manila folder. Although Dad couldn't walk in a straight line, he also made it to the other side of the room performing this activity. Mom was challenged too since she was in the motorized chair, having to bend to push the ball while not running it over.

Then a sock filled with coins had to be tossed and land in an empty shirt box cover. Several attempts were allowed to guarantee success for all.

Finally, everyone had to blow up a balloon. All of us, now "child-like", had fun creating sounds as the air from the balloons escaped. Of course we had to tie off the balloons for our parents. Everyone was a "winner" and received a piece of chocolate and the coins from the sock toss. The demented parents didn't know one coin from the other, or how to make change, but they were thrilled to have money in their pockets and felt like they had won the lottery.

Isolation/In the Dark

Starting in the early afternoons, Dad began closing the blinds, and asking Mom if it was time for bed. This was upsetting to her as she didn't want to be closed up in a dark house. She was constantly running behind Dad, reopening the blinds. Dad wanted to sit in the dark, not seeing glare, shadows or reflections which seemed to scare and disturb him. It had been the same with Stan's parents.

Dad exhibited "sundowning", the term used to refer to increased agitation and wandering during the night. He also started exhibiting the same behavior during the day, wandering and fidgeting, as if he should be working and actively doing something.

How to Occupy His Time

Dad was now in the eighth year of this terrible disease. How to pass the day and not be totally bored was a problem. On the suggestion of a friend, I bought a set of wooden blocks to see if it might be something Dad could do. He really wasn't interested and after three minutes he had enough of that activity. At least he didn't throw the blocks, hurt anyone, or break anything in the house.

The best way to keep Dad occupied was to assign him "jobs" which made him feel useful. He had always been, and still remained, Mom's helper. Dad could pick up things from the floor because Mom couldn't bend down easily to get them. He could retrieve canned goods from the kitchen shelves that were beyond her reach. He helped her carry groceries into the house. He filled the bird feeder with seed and put the garbage can at the curb for pickup.

These activities typically only took 20 minutes to complete. That left a long period of time to fill during the remainder of the day.

For a while, Dad could assist Mom making the bed. He could transfer the laundry from the washer to the dryer. Often, Dad sat on the living room couch watching Mom prepare dinner in the adjoining kitchen. My parents had a lightweight, self-propelled vacuum cleaner. Dad could hold up the cord to the vacuum cleaner while Mom moved the cleaner around the room and help prevent the cord from getting tangled in her motorized chair. Mom used a long handled extension duster to clean pictures, door frames and light fixtures beyond her normal reach.

Mom and I tried to keep Dad physically active. He had begun shuffling and dragging his feet. We had him perform the same exercises Olivia had learned in the Balance Class. We told Dad to pick up his feet when he walked, but this was a signal to him to bend his knees and lift them very high in a strange movement like he was marching in the Army. He no longer knew how to walk normally.

Since Dad had trouble understanding, we had to speak very slowly and clearly. We had to be sure he was looking directly at us. Only one person could speak at a time or it was too confusing for him. Even then, Dad might catch the first word or two, the rest would be lost. Often, our words were misinterpreted.

Dad still loved going to church, even though he didn't understand any of the sermon or scriptures. He still knew some of the hymns by heart and sang along. He always felt he belonged in church, but it was becoming increasingly difficult for Mom to get them both out the door to attend services.

Mom's mobility issues were a big challenge: getting herself and Dad up, dressed and fed, then getting both in and out of the vehicle, walking the distance from the parking lot into the church, making it through the service, and then repeating the process returning home. If it was raining, Mom and Dad didn't dare venture out because of the risks with slippery pavement, shoes and falling.

Lost in the House

Dad was getting lost in the house. Mom now had to give him directions to all the rooms. Sometimes he wound up in a closet and panicked, not able to find his way out. He would yell for help. He got to the bathroom but didn't know where he was or how to get out. He would sit on the toilet and cry until Mom came to rescue him. It was very tragic.

Dad could no longer help with the laundry because he couldn't find the laundry room. I put brightly colored tape on one edge of the doorways to try and assist Dad in locating different rooms. It didn't help.

Loss of Senses

Alzheimer's affects all your senses - vision, hearing, taste, smell and touch.

Even though Dad claimed he couldn't see, he found tiny specks of fuzz on the carpet which he would pick up all day. It was one of his repetitive activity symptoms.

Dad lost all sense of morning and night, couldn't tell time on the clock and had no concept of minutes or hours passing. I located a talking clock which announced the time. If Dad could only remember to push the button! He pushed the button many times during the night, awakening Mom from her sleep. Dad did have actual issues with his sight, but with the Alzheimer's, he saw but did not comprehend what he saw.

Dad panicked if Mom went anywhere, always afraid she wasn't coming back. I tried to explain that she would return when the big hand got to the top of the clock. I pointed to it, but that meant nothing to him. Dad immediately forgot and fretted. I'd repeat the clock visual over and over, finally moving to a different activity to relieve his distress.

Dad no longer knew how to operate his hearing aids. Mom had to check the batteries each day and put them in his ears. Even with the aids in, though he could hear, he could not make sense of the words or their meaning.

Dad had long ago lost his taste for food, except for sweets. Now he only enjoyed eating ice cream, desserts and chocolate. He was reluctant to eat anything else. Mom started giving him chocolate Ensure to drink so he would at least get some nutrients.

The Alzheimer's group suggested putting sugar on all food if that kept the patient eating. Luckily, Dad was not diabetic. He was the opposite of Stan's mother. She would eat everything in sight, while Dad had to be forced to eat.

Scared and Clinging

Mostly, Dad was scared and wanted to hold Mom's hand all day long and not be left alone. **He just wanted love, hugs and to feel safe.** He pleaded with her not to "throw him away". Meanwhile, she was trying to do chores in the house and couldn't always just sit with Dad and give him her total attention.

Dad reminded me of my son, who at age two would cry and hang onto my leg for dear life when he knew I would be leaving him for a short time. In the same way, Mom was

Dad's security blanket. He was trying to hang on and needed comfort. He was following her everywhere. Mom couldn't even manage to go to the bathroom by herself in peace!

Hallucinations

Like Olivia, hearing knocking on her door and seeing midgets, Dad was also experiencing auditory and visual hallucinations. He often reached up and claimed to see people, dogs, birds, flowers and bushes on the ceiling. Mom and I told him it must be very beautiful. At other times, Dad said there were hundreds of mice running around in the house with a cat chasing them. That must have been disconcerting. He also said a brown dog was walking alongside me.

Dad claimed he was talking to his dead brother. Mom and I never argued with Dad or disputed what he believed he saw or heard. Who was I to say whether there was some connection between this world and the next and he was actually communicating with his brother? It was reality to Dad.

Often Dad said there were lots of other people in the room. Later he'd ask us where everyone went. Again, I thought perhaps he might actually be seeing dead people.

Dad seemed to believe that whatever he saw on television (i.e., flooding somewhere in the country) was also happening right in his house, just as my mother-in-law had on 9/11. So Dad was often alarmed and terrified. Just as a young child who has nightmares needs comfort, Dad needed assurance that all was well.

Sometimes, he thought the walls and ceiling were caving in and water was rising in the house. He insisted he and Mom leave and get to higher ground. Mom would reassure him that everything was fine. He was safe.

Since most of the news on television was violence, war, accidents or natural disasters, I suggested to Mom that they watch only channels which would not upset Dad – maybe old Hallmark channel movies or National Geographic. He could not discern what was real versus what was fiction, or whether any threat he saw on TV could actually harm him.

Increased Personal Care

Dad rebelled at shower-time and now had to be bathed and dressed by Mom. He would insist he just had a bath when it had really been three or four days earlier. Mom could only manage to get Dad in the shower once a week. The rest of the time she resorted to baby wipes or sponge baths in the bed. Providing Dad's personal care was no small feat for Mom due to her handicap. Doing anything was difficult from the motorized chair. Not being able to reach or bend increased the difficulty for her, especially if Dad didn't want to cooperate. It took all morning for Mom to get herself and Dad up and dressed. Typically, it was noon before both were ready for breakfast. The day was half over.

Mom really had her hands full with caregiving. As I was the only surviving child in the family and I had only one child living out of state, there was no other immediate family for Mom to rely on for help. I was working full-time, so I couldn't be there during the day and I had limited time on the weekends. There were no other relatives, nieces or nephews nearby either.

Mom and I knew someone who worked at a Memory Care facility in town. He came to my parents' house several times to give Dad a bath and to sit with him for a few hours, giving Mom a break. Dad did not seem upset by someone else providing his care, as long as Mom was still present.

Mom and I secured several names of potential caregivers from the local Senior Citizens Center. Most of these volunteers were elderly themselves and we didn't think they would be able to handle Dad.

Mom really was not comfortable having anyone else alone in their house with Dad. She didn't know how Dad would react, or how the caregiver would react to Dad's outbursts.

Mom also had a distrust of people, as Stan and I had with the in-laws' care. She was afraid the caregivers might go through her personal information or steal possessions if they were alone in the house with just Dad.

Nudity Phase

In the last six months of his disease, Dad began disrobing. Once Dad went into the closet, took off his clothes and refused to come out. Mom couldn't get in there with her motorized chair. The neighbor was summoned for help. He finally persuaded Dad to come out and to put some clothes back on.

Other times, while sitting in the living room or dining room, Dad would take off his belt, then his pants, or try to get out of his shirt. If Dad tried to dress himself, he would get all tangled up in the clothes. Pants and shirts would be on backwards. Dad would be totally frustrated. He could no longer button buttons or zip zippers. I bought him several pair of inexpensive pull on pants with elastic waistbands.

Mom and Dad's neighbors were a big support. Dad could no longer manage the garbage or the mail and Mom couldn't drag the big garbage can. The neighbor started putting the garbage at the curb on collection days and bringing the mail from the mailbox to my parents' door. The neighbor also came over almost every day just to chat and check that everything was OK.

This kindness was a great comfort to me knowing someone was so close by who cared for my parents and could be there immediately in an emergency until I could arrive. These neighbors' parents were deceased so they "adopted" our family. Mom and Dad were now their Mom and Dad, I became their sister, and Stan became their brother.

Dad on the Wait List

Dad started saying he should "leave" and didn't want to be here anymore. Mom thought Dad meant he wanted to go into a nursing home because he was unhappy being locked in the house and he was upset with her. When Mom asked him if that's where he wanted to go, Dad said he didn't know. I interpreted his statement to mean that he, like Olivia, didn't want to be alive in this world in his current condition.

It was obvious that Dad was getting worse and around this time I put my father on a wait list for the Memory floor at a nice care facility in town. They had beds for 50 people in the Memory wing and were in the process of adding another building to accept more memory care and full care patients within six months. Mom hadn't come to grips with placing Dad anywhere, but I told her it was a contingency plan and we weren't committed to anything.

Dad was 5th on the list which meant a wait of several months to a year. I felt we needed to be prepared if moving Dad became a necessity. All that was required was a $500 deposit to put Dad's name on the list, and the deposit would be refunded if circumstances changed and he never entered the facility. There would be no money lost.

Changing Medications and No Sleep

Soon it became obvious that the Namenda prescription wasn't helping Dad in his daily functions. An Exelon patch (for mild to moderate dementia) was administered, along with the drug Ativan (for anxiety and depression). When the Exelon didn't seem to improve Dad's condition, the doctor put him back on Namenda at an increased dosage. Dad also began Seroquel (an anti-psychotic and sleep aid) to help with his sundowning symptoms.

There are many possible side effects from all of these medications, one including dizziness and muscle weakness, resulting in falls. All needed close monitoring. I felt like Dad was a guinea pig, the doctor experimenting to find any drug which might help him.

The first night of this change in medication, Dad fell five times and was highly agitated. He stayed awake for three days - neither he nor Mom got any sleep. I got frantic calls at work to come **HELP!!!** My mother needed a break and time to rest. More calls were made to the doctor. He took Dad off the prescription, but then Dad stayed in bed all day. He only ate 2-3 spoonfuls of food. None of the drugs seemed to provide any improvement in his condition. Some of them seemed to make him worse.

Loss of Communication but Still Praising God

It became increasingly hard for us to follow Dad's train of thought. Things were getting all jumbled together and he had lost the ability to find words or speak in complete sentences. However he would occasionally burst into a line from the *Hallelujah Chorus*, or parts of *God Be With You Til We Meet Again.* Sometimes he would sing or recite sections of the "Lords Prayer", over and over, or he might start speaking Spanish, which he excelled at in high school. Then he started making up little child-like rhymes and laugh at himself. The Alzheimer's patient exhibits behavior and motor skills inverse to a child's development (reverting back to birth, sometimes referred to as retrogenesis). Dad was like a small child.

It was comical and relieving when Dad suddenly burst out singing. He was usually serious, trying hard to recall something he still remembered. So Mom and I began to join with him, singing parts of the *Hallelujah Chorus*. I'm sure, if anyone had walked in on the three of us, they would have thought we were all insane.

Now, remembering this, I realize how devoted and loving to God, Dad remained. Despite the disease Dad was battling, he never blamed God or stopped loving Him. Instead, he prayed continually and praised His Father. Dad's faith was ingrained deeply in his soul, his spirit. I believe this is what helped him overcome his trial to the end of his life.

Music Therapy

Dad sang in church choirs for years. Music was still something he loved and remembered and was a way for him to communicate. Often, Mom put on music and Dad could sit and enjoy it. Sometimes, he tried to sing along or at the very least clap to the beat.

Music activates both the left and right side of the brain. It can improve the mood of a patient and boost cognitive skills. Music is a way to keep people engaged. They can express their emotions and feelings and can interact socially with the caregiver. Music can decrease agitation and help with motor skills through movement.

Early in my career, I was a music teacher in the public schools. I saw the positive benefits of music on emotionally and neurologically impaired students. I also sang in nursing homes and to the house-bound during the holidays. The pleasure of the elderly in hearing well-loved Christmas carols was apparent. Even if they couldn't sing along, they swayed, clapped, or at least smiled. In most, it brought back happy memories of their childhoods. Care facilities usually have music engagement activities and music programs during the year for the residents to enjoy.

I saw the effect of music on my own elderly parents. By listening to music, my mother was brought out of her fog in the hospital. My in-laws were calmed by listening to soft music, and brought to life listening to songs of their era. My father-in-law heard soft music to reduce pain during his final day in comfort care. My mother-in-law was able to speak the last 5 words of a song sung by Stan. My father could sing some lyrics and respond by clapping to the rhythm of music he heard. Any response meant their brains were still working and being stimulated.

Music is one of the first things we hear as children. Parents may sing us lullabies. Children sing nursery rhymes in school. At the end of life, hearing sounds and appreciating music appear to be one of the last abilities to be lost. The person comes full circle, back to a beginning.

Even a patient who cannot sing can tap a foot or sway to the beat. One needn't be a talented singer or instrumentalist to participate in the miracle of music. Give your loved one a pot and a spoon, or beatable cardboard box. They can use arms, pretending to conduct an orchestra. The possibilities are endless. I cannot think of one person who does not enjoy music in some fashion.

Stress and At Battle

As the months passed, life became even more stressful for Mom. She was worn-out and depressed about the whole Alzheimer's situation and was quickly losing patience with Dad. They were often "at battle" with one another.

Mom and Dad would fight over control of the covers in bed at night. Dad would pull off all the blankets and sheets, throw everything on the floor, leaving Mom awake, freezing and mad. He was getting all tangled up in the blankets and said they were "too heavy" and bothered his feet.

Mom tried switching to very light-weight covers, but Dad still had an issue. It seemed that anything touching his body: sheets, blankets or clothing, felt too confining or restrictive. He felt smothered and wanted them all gone. The dementia affected this sensory perception.

Mom was at her wits end and was snapping at Dad more often. He too was frustrated with himself for not being able to do things anymore. He couldn't understand what was going on and was so confused. Result: an outburst.

As much as our hearts were always trying to do what was best for Dad and to help him, he couldn't comprehend our true meaning and purpose. As an example, Dad was barely eating or drinking and starting to lose considerable weight. He was becoming malnourished and in a "failure to thrive" state (FTT). He had lost more than 5% of his previous normal weight. Mom would say "YOU HAVE TO EAT" (meaning in order to stay alive). To Dad, that was yelling and forcing him to do something he didn't want to. He didn't feel hunger any more and nothing had a taste.

Additionally, trying to eat was an overwhelming task for Dad. He had to find the correct utensil to use, remember how to lift it, how to maneuver food onto it, then find his mouth, and finally, remember how to chew and swallow. It was an unending cycle of anxiety and frustration for him.

Larger handled silverware was somewhat helpful, as were rimmed dishes which kept the food on the plate as Dad pushed it around. Also, a solid colored tablecloth and solid colored plate were less distracting and helped him locate the food he was supposed to be eating. Still, he barely ate a few bites.

Soon, Dad lost the ability to swallow and started choking during meals. Mom disciplined herself to silence, so Dad could concentrate on eating and not feel compelled to converse.

Search for Care Facility Openings

Mom was growing increasingly desperate and unable to care for Dad alone, but still reluctant to admit it. I again contacted numerous local facilities to inquire if any might have an opening for him. Of the 10 facilities I called regarding placement, I was told there were no openings, but Dad was added on wait lists at three.

The staff at these facilities said it was very difficult to place a man in memory or full care. The reason? More women lived longer than men. The former could easily be paired together in a room, whereas a man could not share a room with a woman. Rarely are there private rooms in a facility. I never realized how difficult it would be to get placed. The overwhelming demand was far greater than the number of rooms available anywhere.

Over the previous 13 years, I had researched 20 facilities within a 30 mile radius, personally visiting 15 of them, as the level of need for our loved ones changed. Some facilities only had Assisted Living, some had SCALF, some were primarily for rehab, some were full nursing homes and a few had assisted living, SCALF and full care wings.

I created a spreadsheet with pertinent information and my rating including pros and cons of each facility. In even the highest rated rehab/care facility, an acquaintances brother had escaped from lock-down for a few hours. Another acquaintance reported that she had witnessed "rough handling" of a patient. This increased my uneasiness about placing Dad anywhere.

The nicest Life Care facility charged a basic entrance fee when you were in good health. The patient would move to different levels throughout the remainder of life as needs increased. **<u>Many of these facilities do not accept people who already have a developing dementia,</u>** so those were removed from the potential placement list.

A few of the full care nursing homes I visited looked terrible and had such a strong smell of urine that they were immediately crossed off the list for consideration as well. Most patients' rooms were tiny, with just enough space for a single bed, and a small clothes closet.

Bathroom Issues

Because Dad was drinking only a few sips of liquid a day, he began to have bathroom issues. Poor Mom had to monitor Dad's bowel movements much like a child first learning to use the potty. After going, he had to call her in to "inspect" what he had done and she tracked it on the calendar. He had bowel impaction numerous times, be totally stopped up and in pain, which mandated the dreaded "BLASTER TREATMENT" - a combination of the doctors' prescription for Lactulose (laxative), plus hot prune juice and suppositories. Several times, Mom had to manually dig it out to prevent a trip to the emergency room. Going there would have been even more stressful and traumatic for both parents.

Safety Concerns and Out of Control Behavior

Dad began getting combative and his doctor tried different medications to no avail. There was a drastic change in Dad's behavior. He had always been so kind and easy-going. Always a gentle spirit. Mom kept asking the doctor's office what else could be done, as she was really getting desperate. She was told that if Dad got out of control, she should call 911, the police would come and take Dad to the hospital. He would be admitted, evaluated, stabilized and then moved to a care facility.

Dad told Mom he was in hell and wanted a knife so he could kill himself. He did not want live in his mentally and physically declined condition. It became a big safety issue and Mom now had to watch Dad even more closely.

Dad was moving furniture around the living and dining room, hitting Mom with his shoe, spitting out food, and tossing hot coffee at her. He was up at night wandering and dragging bedding around the house, throwing CD's on the floor and causing general havoc.

This behavior, and all the clean-up, was extremely difficult and upsetting for Mom. I don't know how she kept it together. Dealing with Stan's mother was overwhelming for me but I was younger and able-bodied for all the clean-up. Mom had her own handicap, making everything a challenge and very time consuming, even under normal circumstances.

One day, Dad raised his hand as if he were holding a gun and pretended to shoot Mom. Now safety escalated from Dad harming himself to him potentially harming Mom – even though they had no guns. I was so worried.

Mom felt like Dad was threatening her and was afraid of him. That night she parked her motorized chair, blocking the hallway, in order to protect herself. She slept in a recliner in another room.

Stan and I had heard from others in the Alzheimer's support group that the patient often becomes hostile toward their caregivers at some point. This appeared to be what was happening with Dad.

Dad also started knocking things down, turning over our pictures, so Mom and I had to childproof the house. We guessed that since Dad didn't recognize us anymore in the pictures, he thought some strangers were in the room watching him. It made him suspicious and fearful.

Babbling and Unable to Feed Self – Full Care Status

Soon Dad started babbling and not making any sense. Mom was managing to get a few spoonfuls of food into his mouth most of the time. There were rare occasions when Dad could still lift a spoon by himself or manage simple finger foods. This was a big problem. In order to get into Memory Care ***you had to be ambulatory,*** even if it was pushing yourself with your feet while in a wheelchair. ***You also had to be able to feed yourself***. One could rarely get into full care without first coming from Memory Care or coming directly from the hospital or a rehab facility.

After a few weeks of this behavior, and Mom's and my increased desperation, I called the local facility where I had put a deposit down for Dad. They told me there was now an opening in Memory Care. Mom and I took Dad for the doctors' write-up and chest x-rays. The x-rays were a challenge because Dad could not follow any directions about how to sit. However the technician finally managed to get the photos taken.

Reviewing Dad's test results, the doctor said the pockets in Dad's lungs were collapsing, but that was normal for someone his age (95-1/2 years old). He found nothing to prevent Dad's admittance to the facility.

Next, Mom and I took Dad to the care facility itself, for their evaluation. We informed them that Dad needed to be bathed and dressed but that he could still feed himself "somewhat". Luckily, the evaluators stepped out of the room before Dad became very agitated and began moving their furniture around.

Dad barely passed the evaluation for admittance and the facility commented that they would have to see when Dad arrived, whether he could remain at that level of care. I was worried because another friend of mine had a mother-in-law in a SCALF and when her condition declined, the facility gave the family just two weeks to have the mother-in-law removed and find full care.

A few days later, Stan and I set up Dad's room at the care facility in preparation of taking him there. We moved in a bed, a dresser, a night table, a sitting chair, and some pictures. The facility utilized an outside pharmacy to fill Dad's prescriptions, which were prepared and individually bubble-wrapped for security.

We knew that if Dad proved "unsuitable" for Memory Care, despite a full-care wing on the premises, a long wait list precluded that replacement. If Dad got to that point, Mom and I would have to find another full care facility for Dad or bring him back home. At that time, I had not received any call-backs from the other three facilities Dad was wait-listed on. It didn't look promising for any options.

Geriatric Psychiatric Hospital

The afternoon Stan and I arrived at my parents' house to take Dad to Memory Care, Dad collapsed…with me holding him up, then gently lowering him to the floor. I thought perhaps he had suffered a heart attack. Mom called 911 and Dad was taken to the hospital. There we all sat for seven hours, while numerous tests and scans were performed. They said Dad was dehydrated, but they couldn't admit him because the hospital was full. Also, they did not want him exposed to all the other people with the flu and pneumonia - it would be a great risk to him.

Dad was totally combative. Even after three shots of valium in the emergency room, <u>it took five of us</u> to hold him down and get his clothes back on to take him home. Once back home, Dad only slept an hour and a half. The rest of the night he was up causing his usual havoc.

The next morning, arriving at my parents' house, Mom was crying. She said she couldn't live like this any longer. It was obvious to me that she could no longer cope with the situation. There needed to be some other solution. My greatest concern now was for her own health and sanity. Dad had to be removed from the house.

Since the hospital wouldn't admit Dad, and he could no longer be accepted by Memory Care - his combative behavior was judged a danger to residents and staff - Stan and I had only one other option. It was the geriatric psychiatric hospital that I had learned of through the Alzheimer's Association.

Mom was struggling with this as she felt responsible for Dad's care. After all, he had taken care of her through her many physical ailments. I think, in bringing Dad to this facility, Mom felt she had failed him, "thrown him away". Also, she was fearful about the care he might receive. I tried to reassure her. She had done a truly amazing job with Dad's care in extremely traumatic circumstances, but now Dad needed more help than either of us could provide.

Luckily, I had already bought Dad clothes acceptable in a facility: no belts, ties, or anything with strings which could be a danger to the patient or others. Dad had slip-on, rubber-soled shoes and stretchable waistband pants. He could have nothing of value, such as jewelry - only his glasses, dentures and hearing aids. The facility would not even allow toothpaste or soap, as a dementia patient might not know what to do with these and wind up ingesting the product.

Mom, Stan and I were able to get Dad in the car and to the facility by telling him he was going to see the doctor. We left out the fact that he was going to stay there by himself for a little while.

After the nurse's initial review of Dad, and write-up of important information, it was time for us to go. It was very difficult leaving Dad. He was crying. Mom and I told him that the doctors were trying to help by adjusting his medications and we would be back to see him. I really hoped they could stabilize his behavior and then he could either come home, or go to the Memory Care facility.

The psychiatric hospital was totally "lock-down". Mom and I gained access in and out of the building by the staff that controlled the doors.

Dad continued to go downhill at this facility – hitting, kicking, biting and spitting at the caregivers and masturbating. These actions were part of his brain disease and deterioration, also a defense mechanism toward strangers' actions and needing to do something which brought comfort.

Dad was severely dehydrated. The doctors tried to keep him on constant IV's, but Dad would pull out the needles. The facility said strapping a patient down was a last resort because it was so very traumatic.

Dad was severely malnourished and had pneumonia. He could no longer feed himself, couldn't walk, could barely stand, and had to have assistance to transfer from the chair to the bed. He was now in a totally helpless, baby-like state.

Dad continued to take off his clothes. This was a big issue at the facility, because if he did that in the visitation area when other patients' family members were present, Dad would have to be removed and our visit with him would be over. Mom and I spent much of our visiting time trying to hold Dad's pants up, while he tried to pull them down.

The staff suggested giving Dad something to hold. I brought him a soft, stuffed bear of mine that he held. The bear kept his hands occupied and his pants on.

The facility then provided Dad with a Gerichair which was very foamy and cushioned to prevent pressure sores. He stayed in a reclined position, feet raised, so no risk of him getting up. It was virtually impossible for him to remove his clothes in that chair, or do much of anything.

The facility allowed only two hours of visitation late in the afternoon. Fortunately my employer allowed me to work shorter days to be able to see Dad during that time. I used vacation hours to make up the difference.

Mom was uneasy with the facility because they didn't allow visitors in the patient's room and Mom thought they were hiding something. But, as the rooms were shared, and all the patients had psychiatric problems, I could understand why the facility had that rule.

The regular doctor and the psychiatrist evaluated Dad daily. Mom and I had several joint consultations with the total staff regarding Dad's treatment and progress, or lack thereof. I felt they were doing everything possible, but it was a losing battle because Dad was in the very final stage of the disease and nothing was going to help. Mom thought that Dad's decline was somehow the facility's fault and she was not satisfied with them. She said she hoped I never put her there.

Sometimes Dad was brought to the visiting room in someone else's clothes. His glasses were missing and one hearing aid broken. Mom and I started questioning the care he was receiving and the lack of care for his personal items. Since the rooms were shared, it was possible that Dad's roommate or other patients were the cause of the issues.

Dad was no longer wearing his dentures. They didn't fit correctly due to major weight loss and they irritated his mouth. He was just gumming food. The facility asked Mom and I to try to feed Dad. He wasn't eating for them. We brought soft foods Dad had still enjoyed more recently at home. But even when I tried to feed Dad, he took a few spoonfuls then spit out the rest all over me. He couldn't handle the texture of food anymore and his ability to swallow had grown worse.

Dad could say only a word or two now. Occasionally, his eyes were open, but he would look up toward the ceiling and not focus on Mom or me. Other times, his eyes were closed, but once he tried to sing along with us to a familiar song. When I asked Dad if our singing was good, he just shrugged his shoulders. He still understood a little.

The medications the facility experimented with seemed to be of no help, and after three weeks they could no longer keep Dad. Mom and I had to decide on placing him elsewhere or bring him home.

End of Life Care Decision

After Dad was diagnosed with pneumonia for a second time, his doctor at the geriatric hospital told Mom and me that pneumonia would continually plague my father. And then, he added that according to his estimation, Dad had one month to live. Mom and I needed to make an end of life care decision and it would be gut-wrenching.

We visited several full care facilities. Happily, the one we liked best was also the closest one to Mom's house. But even that drive would be a trial for her. Also, she would be very uncomfortable sitting there for hours – with minimal privacy – but lots of time to ponder Dad's care (or lack thereof) when she was absent.

Every facility visited claimed to "check" on patients every two hours, but both Mom and I believed that probably meant a staff member would simply confirm that Dad was still alive, doing little else for his well-being. The full care facilities claimed to average one caregiver for every eight patients. Mom and I felt they could not possibly provide the individual attention that Dad needed.

We already knew, after Mom's experience in rehab, that she could be left for hours before anyone came to change her. She had been in one of the highest rated facilities and she had all her mental faculties! We did not want to think about Dad being at anyone's mercy in his state.

In addition, the facility we were considering for Dad required an initial week of rehab before he could be moved to the full care area (provided there was a timely opening). This rehab requirement was, to us, a useless and cruel experience for Dad to endure.

Even after learning that Dad's internist and his psychiatric hospital doctor both made rounds to this facility, I remained ambivalent. Would that I could leave my job, even temporarily, but this would be impossible. Stan, who was not working at the time, and I needed my full salary for bills and mortgage payment.

Mom and I were also greatly concerned about the cost of the full care facility, especially if Dad lingered on. My friend's mother-in-law lived a full year bedridden and helpless. Medicare would pay 100% of the first 21 days. Then there would be a co-pay of $165/day for the next 90 days. ***But dementia is usually not considered to warrant Medicare coverage in a skilled nursing facility***. Mom was expecting to have to pay the total care cost.

A friend of our family told me that if Dad went in a facility, they would not take my parents home or my mothers Social Security, but they would take Dad's Social Security as well as all of my parents' savings. Once that money was gone, Medicaid relief could be applied for to cover ongoing care.

Mom determined that she could afford to pay a maximum of eight months for Dad's full care. Beyond that, she would have insufficient remaining funds for her own future. She required more than just her social security to make ends meet and she didn't want to sell their house.

I heard about people trying to "hide" their assets from a care facility and "spend down" their money; perhaps purchasing a new car, redoing a kitchen or signing over a house to a child. But there is a five year "look back" rule enabling a facility the right to peruse all spending and possibly disqualifying Medicaid coverage. Interestingly, a child may be "gifted" $10,000 a year without question.

To Die at Home

After much discussion, Mom and I finally decided to bring Dad home with Hospice care. We would not place him in any rehab/full care facility. Stan and I cleared out Dad's study to make room for the hospital bed which Hospice would bring.

We called the Memory Care facility and told them Dad would not be coming there. Stan and I retrieved the furniture we had previously moved in and the facility reimbursed Mom the fee she had paid for the first month of care.

The psychiatric hospital transported Dad home, and Mom and I were left on our own. For some reason there was confusion about Dad's actual release day and time. The Hospice nurse didn't arrive immediately.

When I first checked Dad, I found he had had severe diarrhea running down both legs and even into his socks. Mom could barely stand herself and was unable to maneuver Dad for a change, so changing detail became my job. It was not a question of doing it - it had to be done. There was no way Mom could have cared for Dad at this stage by herself.

Mom called Hospice and the nurse came but was unable to get any vitals because of Dad's continued combativeness and inability to follow instructions. As soon as he moved, the readings would Error out. Hospice supplied diapers, mattress protector pads, cleaning lotions and creams. They also brought an oxygen tank and provided instructions, however Dad's breathing never seemed labored so I never used it. I had to buy additional diapers and mattress protectors because we ran out of supplies before Hospice replenished them.

Home care assistance from a local provider would not start until the agency could line up caregivers for the hours Mom wanted. So I left my home once again and moved into my parents' house to care for Dad.

I struggled trying to turn Dad over, to wipe and change him. He hung onto the hospital bed rails, not cooperating. It was surprising how strong he still was, even without eating much and having pneumonia. I finally discovered how to get him to turn, by telling him I wanted to give him a hug. That way he held onto me instead of the bed rail.

Mom and I started a journal, noting everything Dad ate and drank, the times we administered his medications, when he was changed and all other care information.

Thank goodness my boss continued to be so understanding and supportive. My employer was agreeable to a flexible work schedule. I still had a little vacation and sick time available too. If not for all this, I don't know what I would have done about my job and I'm glad I didn't have to make that decision. Quitting wasn't an option. I would have had to take money from my 401k to pay bills and it would have severely decreased my future social security benefits and adversely affected retirement plans.

I was able to help Dad and still get on-line to do office work at various hours of the day and night. Keeping up with work was actually a good distraction for me. It was a respite from the otherwise constant depressive care situation at hand.

The home aides finally came the next week, but once Dad was changed, several did nothing but sit, do homework or talk on cell phones. Mom had to pay the care agency a minimum of four hours per visit at a rate of $17/hour. A caregiver came from 8am-12 noon, then another came from 6-10 pm before bed.

There were three caregivers who took out the garbage, vacuumed the house, and cleaned the floor – but those things didn't need to be done every day. Most of them wound up sitting and talking to Mom and me.

There was a surprise blessing in all of this. The Hospice nurse belonged to Mom and Dad's church and the Hospice chaplain had been the previous chaplain at their church. In addition, when the Hospice social worker arrived, she was the social worker who previously worked for DHR and had helped with Stan's parents' situation. She gave Mom and I a guide outlining the end-of-life signs to watch for. This was very helpful. The Hospice nurse came every few days and a Hospice caregiver came to sponge bathe Dad daily. As Dad declined further, the nurse came more frequently to get vitals and evaluate his condition.

A friend of ours worked for the home care agency and Mom was able to secure some of her time to help with Dad. That was another familiar face and support. It seemed like Divine intervention. People we knew and trusted were there to help us at the end of Dad's life. God was looking out for us.

We were told that Hospice would provide 11 hours of caregiving once a month if needed. I do not remember being informed of that when Olivia was initially under Hospice care.

Dad was on Remeron (mirtazapine) to treat major depression and four anti-psychotic/mood stabilizers (including Geodan), for his behavioral issues. The doctors had tried to find something that would alleviate the symptoms of his dying brain.

During the first week at home, Dad was able to take a few bites of soft food or drink – yogurt, applesauce, pureed foods, ice cream, pudding, Ensure, or broth – enough to get his pills down. I praised him for trying and doing such a good job. He responded with <u>one last smile</u>, but no longer remembered how to speak. The loss of communication was the most troubling, because now Dad couldn't tell us if anything was wrong.

The Last Two Weeks

Four days later, Dad seemed to be in ever-increasing pain and I noticed he was bleeding a lot in his diaper. I decided it was probably due to a urinary tract infection, but I never saw that much blood before and it was quite alarming. I changed Dad every hour as he cried out in pain "Momma", while passing blood and large clots. Antibiotics were started.

Dad began to raise his arms upward, as if he were receiving a blessing, or trying to catch and hold on to something. Mom asked, "Are you seeing beautiful flowers, someone you loved and lost?" Of course, at this point, Dad couldn't answer.

A day later, Dad could no longer swallow at all. The pills just sat on his tongue. Because he continued to appear in pain, Hospice agreed to prescribe morphine which would be administered by drops.

Two unusual snow storms hit our area. I could barely make the trip to and from the pharmacy on the icy roads and with road closures. Then there was a mix-up with the prescription. Waiting for approval meant Dad would have to hang in there longer for the pain relief he needed.

I now experienced the same desperation for my father as I had experienced with my brother at the end of his life. When he was in the hospital dying of cancer, which had spread throughout his entire body, he asked, "Why does it hurt so much?" I pleaded with the nurse to give him more morphine. She said it wasn't possible; he had received a dose not long ago. I felt so helpless. It was a terrible thing seeing my loved ones in pain.

After a day of morphine drops, given every four hours and absorbed through the inside of the cheek, Dad's pain seemed to subside. But Mom and I knew that without food or water, his life was coming to an end. I didn't think Dad had felt hungry for a long time, nor did he thirst, but I prayed he was not suffering.

It had been decided many years earlier, that there would be no valiant efforts to keep either parent alive with feeding tubes. Knowing this, I felt myself switching from daughter (who would love, hurt and hesitate) to nurse. Nurse was a less painful cap to wear. I had to be strong for both parents and provide the care Dad needed.

Dad began looking like a concentration camp victim. He was down to approximately 90 pounds - just skin and bones, eyes sinking in and ribs jutting outward. Sometimes his eyes were partially open but glazed. He did not seem to register anything around him. But if someone was talking in the room, Dad seemed to breathe faster and turn his head as if he were aware of our presence and still heard us. We were told that the last sense to go is hearing. A final grasp of Mom's hand, like a newborn would, was the last sign of Dad sensing anything.

Mom and I played soft music near Dad's bed and sang to him. I put on the sound machine so he could hear the ocean waves he loved or the peaceful rain forest and birds chirping. I described the beautiful snowy scene outside his window that I wished he could see.

Stan couldn't cope with seeing my father in this condition, as he loved him too. He was still grieving from the loss of his mother just a few months earlier and running away from another impending death. He didn't visit much, except at the end of Dad's life. Although there was really nothing Stan could do, I missed having his support there. Every few nights I went home for two hours to have dinner with him and pick up some clean clothes to bring back to my parents' house.

Over the next three days, Dad's breathing slowed down tremendously, **three breaths a minute**. A normal adult takes 12-20 breaths per minute. I would watch and wait, and wait, and wait, all for that next breath. Mom and I took turns administering the morphine, although, since I was sleeping on my parents' couch, I heard every sound, was up every hour at night checking Dad. And I wanted Mom to rest. Dad didn't move or respond at all.

Pressure sores developed all along Dad's body during that last week. His back, bottom and even his hands and fingers began to turn purple, and were covered with sores and blisters from the lack of oxygen. I saw his body decaying daily. I stopped trying to secure his diaper and, instead, draped it over him loosely. There was minimal fluid output since Dad had stopped eating and drinking.

The next day, Dad's breathing changed again. It was fast, but shallow. Mom and I had been telling Dad for days that it was OK to go, that we would be fine and he need not worry about us. Still, I wondered if he understood our assurances.

That afternoon, Mom and I went to the funeral home to select an urn for my father's ashes. Our neighbor sat with Dad, at home.

He Leaves Us

The next morning I went into Dad's room to administer his regular dose of morphine. Then Mom & I sat on each side of the bed, holding Dad's hands. We talked about how wonderful it would be in Heaven. I joked that there would be quite a commotion on his arrival as he would be celebrating with so many friends and relatives.

As if he agreed and was now ready to go, Dad suddenly stopped breathing. He rose up slightly from the bed and opened his mouth twice, as if to say something, but I think it was just the last air expelling from his body. Mom and I kept waiting and looking for the next breath, which never came.

Dad died that morning in his own home, with Mom and me at his side, after more than a week without food or water. Witnessing his death was a very profound experience and something I will never forget. I was glad I had traveled this road with him to the end. Mom and Dad had been married for 67 years.

Even the Hospice nurse cried when she saw Dad that final time. She pronounced him dead, bathed him, and released his body to the funeral home. The causes of death were listed as 1) Alzheimer's disease, 2) dementia with behavioral issues (combative), 3) pneumonia and 4) inability to swallow. Dad had gone the full course of the disease and suffered every symptom possible.

We waited two weeks after Dad's death to hold his memorial service. I was in a daze, trying to process all that had happened over the previous decade and a half, caring for the three parents. I am still processing some of it.

After the death of my father, Stan and I went through an empty-nest syndrome. It was an adjustment to suddenly have time to ourselves, to decide how we were going to use it, and be able to become involved again with previous hobbies, with our own social life and with each other.

While I miss Dad's company, intelligence and witty humor more than I could possibly express in words, he lived 95-1/2 wonderful years and was such a blessing to me. Life goes on and I still have my mother to love and care for.

Her outings have further declined. It takes 3 hours to get ready to go out. Standing and walking, even a few steps with a walker, is difficult and exhausting. Although still driving very short distances, back roads are taken - the highway avoided. Maneuvering the motorized chair in and out of her vehicle, while maintaining her balance, is almost impossible alone. During the week she now accepts transportation and assistance to church socials from others in her church circle. More than a year and a half later, we continue to measure time in ADD – life "after Dad's death".

CONCLUSION

As painful as it was for Stan and me to watch the effects of dementia/Alzheimer's on three of our parents: inability to perform simple tasks, reason and make sound decisions, recognize family, see, dress, bathe, read and write, comprehend, taste, walk, stand, speak, eat, swallow, hear, and finally breathe, it was an experience neither of us would have chosen to avoid.

It is certainly not for the weak of faith or stamina. It was so taxing on all family members and totally consumed our lives. It was a daunting role. Sometimes I questioned what the purpose of our parents being alive was, in their state of confusion and total dependence. I came to believe it was to teach me to become a more loving, compassionate and humble person and to better appreciate each day of life; to give thanks if I was physically and mentally well. Also, it encouraged me to discover more about this disease and to help other families who were dealing with it.

In Dad's demented state, a great day for him was when he still knew what a shoe was and could slip it on his foot, when he could pick up a fork and use it, when he could swallow a pill. A fantastic day for him was when he remembered his name, could speak one word, or could still smile. I was taking so many things for granted. What seemed like simple things to me, were great achievements for him and warranted celebration and praise.

To be a great caregiver requires patience, loving kindness, and selflessness. Not everyone can handle caregiving mentally, emotionally and physically.

Part of being able to caregive depends on age, health, and work situation. Can a job be left to care for a loved one full-time? There simply is no easy choice.

Our parents' situations frequently made me feel like there was a heavy weight pulling me down, sucking the life from me. By being bluntly honest about our situation and my feelings, I hope it does not scare you from assuming a caregiving role. While it took a huge toll on me, my husband and my mother, going through these experiences with our loved ones also made us much stronger.

When I felt that I couldn't handle the responsibility anymore, I would try to put myself in my parents' shoes, imagining what they were going through. I prayed that if I ever got dementia, I would have someone to care for me as I was caring for our parents. I loved our family members and knew the wonderful people they had been. Despite their loss of abilities, they still experienced emotions, including happiness and joy, sorrow and pain.

I also continually reminded myself why my father and in-laws were acting as they did. It was <u>the disease</u>. They were upset and frustrated because they had lost their memories and the ability to do anything anymore. They frequently took that frustration out on us, the caregivers.

We were strangers to them now, asking them to do things they didn't understand.

Throughout the years of care that Stan and I provided to our parents, we continually re-evaluated our approaches. We had to be flexible enough to do whatever we thought was in the best interests of everyone involved at any point in time.

We left our own home for a year and moved in with my in-laws. After Stan's father died, we moved his mother to our house. Then we purchased the manufactured home and the three of us moved there. After my mother-in-law died, I moved to my parents' house until my father's death.

At some point, with each loved one, Stan and I believed we needed to find a care facility; but in the end, the care remained for us to provide. It was the right decision for our families as a whole.

The search for potential care options was extremely frustrating. Ultimately, Stan and I wound up juggling the care of the three elderly dementia/Alzheimer's parents ourselves because: 1) we found the care facilities lacking in the quality of care we wanted for our loved ones, 2) the facilities had no openings or long wait lists, 3) the "good" care facilities were not an option for us financially for any long term, and 4) we were disappointed in the quality of other in-home care services and personnel.

Finding a facility that will accept a person with combative dementia seemed non-existent. As with any other person with a mental disease or brain impairment, the patient is often deemed a "problem" that few facilities will handle.

Hopefully, progress can continue to be made to get past the negative perception of those with brain diseases and concentrate on the help that might be provided to keep our loved ones functioning as long as possible. A diagnosis of dementia should be accepted the same as if one were diagnosed with a disease such as cancer or Parkinson's. Families should not be afraid to discuss it and seek help and education.

While research continues, there is still no full understanding of what causes the death and dysfunction of neurons in the brain. If solely a result of one mutated or permanently changed gene inherited from our parents, then my husband will have an almost 100% chance of getting Alzheimer's and I will have a 50% chance.

Many say it is a complex series of events including genetics, plus environmental and lifestyle choices affected by sleep, diet and exercise. Some recent pilot studies tried non-drug treatment programs with patients: avoiding simple carbs, gluten and processed foods, increased intake of fish oil, B12, D3, and melatonin, and practicing yoga and meditation to relieve stress and inflammation. Improvement from these methods showed help in the early stage of dementia, but not later on. Perhaps a combination of drug and non-drug treatment may eventually be the answer. There currently is no proven cure.

Dementia patients **need to feel safe, loved, wanted and useful**. They should be allowed to continue doing as much as they are capable of doing. <u>Praising any achievement</u>, however small it seemed to us, went a long way in maintaining their happiness and dignity. When our parents could no longer do anything, I could still sit with them, hold a hand, give a smile, or offer a word of encouragement. I could do that right to the end of their lives.

It is very important to talk to parents about wills, advanced directives and other living and care arrangements <u>well in advance</u> of any illness. By the time Stan and I started asking questions, his parents were already far into their disease, which caused many complications, the opportunity for abuse, and complicated legal issues. Parents' wills must be updated and include a Living Will regarding medical wishes for end of life care. Someone must be assigned with <u>Durable</u> Power of Attorney for that time when decisions for themselves can no longer be made.

There were times I felt resentful of my circumstance, times I lost patience, times I thought I was being driven crazy and losing my mind right along with my loved ones. And then there was the guilt for feeling my own feelings. These were warning flags for me. I had to remove myself from the situation, even if only for an hour.

Stan and I reversed roles with our parents. We acted as guardians, while they became helpless in grown adult bodies. As a newborn develops, a parent is so excited and proud of each new achievement. When persons suffer from dementia/Alzheimer's, every knowledge gradually disappears. We ***constantly grieved for years*** watching this very slow death process. Although our parents were still in their physical bodies, their minds, memories and abilities vanished one by one.

Besides trying to keep my family members healthy and happy, we had to keep them safe lest they swallow something harmful, fall and hurt themselves, or harm us, the caregivers, when combative or hallucinating.

The same as dealing with any person who has a devastating terminal illness, we, as caregivers, were stretched very thin, and the disease continued for years. I always felt torn between providing care for my in-laws and being with my husband. Torn too, having the responsibility to provide the same quality of care for my own father and to help my mother cope. I was grateful that I was able to devote dedicated care to my father at the end of his life.

Before the final stages, my father and my in-laws all expressed concern, not wanting to be a burden to us. They felt badly that we had been thrown into the legal dilemmas and extreme care issues.

Words of Encouragement and Faith

The years of my journey were quite a challenge, but I was never alone in the caregiving effort. It was only possible through the joint contribution of community resources and the many individuals who were willing to help. We are all extended family.

Would I go through this again? Yes, absolutely. As difficult as it was, my husband and I wanted our parents to have the best individual care possible. That being said, <u>we continually questioned</u> whether we were doing the right thing every step of the way.

I can truly say it was a privilege for me to provide care for our three parents. No one could save them from this disease, but I could provide lots of love during their battle and help make their transition to the next life more pleasant. I like to think of them now, confusion-free and having fun again. I know Dad would want people to be educated about Alzheimer's and understand what he went through. That belief helped me tell this story, in his honor.

I felt God was ever present for me and my family members. I know HE was the one in control of every situation and helping me constantly throughout this journey. Despite the hardships, grief, and feelings of loss, HIS plan was always at work, not only for our loved ones, but for us, the caregivers.

My <u>trust in God</u> and my belief in eternal life was the only way I got through these years. I do not know how someone without faith could emotionally survive witnessing the decline and death of any loved one with a lengthy terminal disease. HE guided me every step of the way and gave me the strength to do what had to be done to help my family.

When you feel like things are hopeless and you can't take the grief any longer, remember that **God loves you. HE will not give you more than you can handle**. If you are going through or have gone through the dementia experience with a loved one, I pray that you find **<u>peace</u> and the confidence in knowing you did your best**.

APPENDIX

Timeline of Alzheimer's Discovery and Research

1906-1969: Discovery – Alois Alzheimer described changes in a patients brain where he saw dramatic shrinkage and abnormal deposits in and around nerve cells. In 1910 the disease was first named and in 1931 the microscope enabled the study of brain cells in greater detail. In 1968 the first measurement scales to assess cognitive and functional decline were developed.

1970-1979: Research – The National Institute on Aging was established as a federal agency which supports Alzheimer's research. In 1976, Alzheimer's was identified as the most common cause of dementia.

1980-1989: Awareness – The Alzheimer's Association was founded and the beta-amyloid protein was identified as the chief component of plaque triggering nerve cell damage and tau protein as a key component of tangles and nerve cell degeneration. In 1987 a gene was identified and associated with inherited forms of Alzheimer'. The first drug to treat symptoms of the disease was used in clinical trials.

1990-1999: Treatments – In 1991 Federal studies began. The first risk factor gene was identified and the first drug approved by the Food and Drug Administration. In 1994 former President Ronald Reagan announced he had been diagnosed with Alzheimer's disease and his wife Nancy Reagan became a strong advocate for research. In 1999 a vaccine proved successful in mice.

2000-2009: Progress – Genetic studies began and an imaging agent for early detection was used along with standards for interpretation. An Alzheimer's journal was launched and actions outlined for the prevention of impairment.

2010-present: National Agenda - Researchers unite to gain awareness and search for funding. A clinical database was established. Alzheimer's is now the sixth leading cause of US deaths. Biomarkers were identified for the disease stages and symptoms. President Obama signed the National Alzheimer's Project Act into law to address the Alzheimer's crisis and coordinate research, care and support. Annual Wellness Visits to assess and detect cognitive impairment and the first major clinical trials for prevention were initiated. New gene risk factors were identified. Rates of death are believed to be much higher than first thought.

Caregiving Aids

Door alarms

Bed rails to help get up

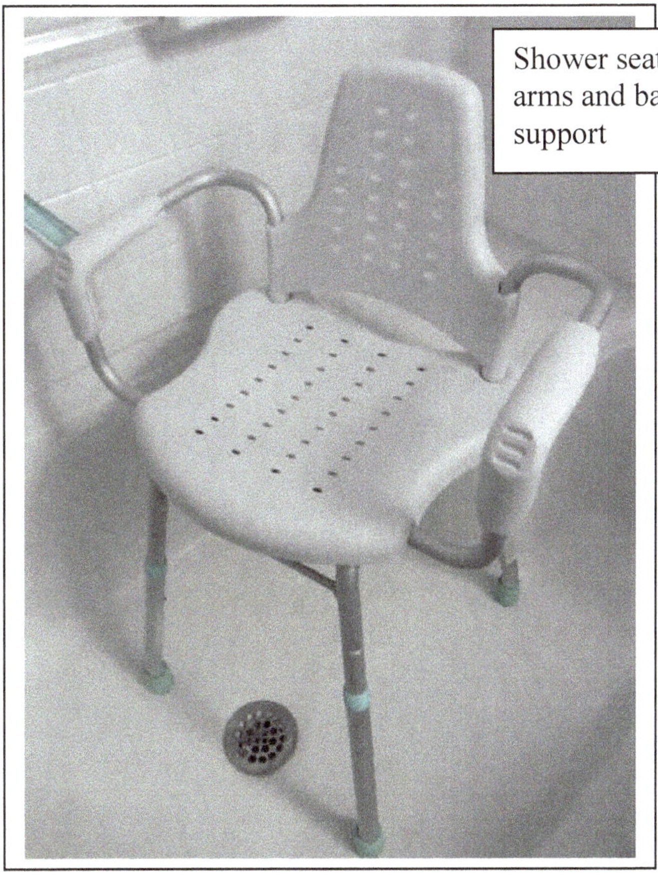

Shower seat with arms and back support

Bars for outside and inside the shower

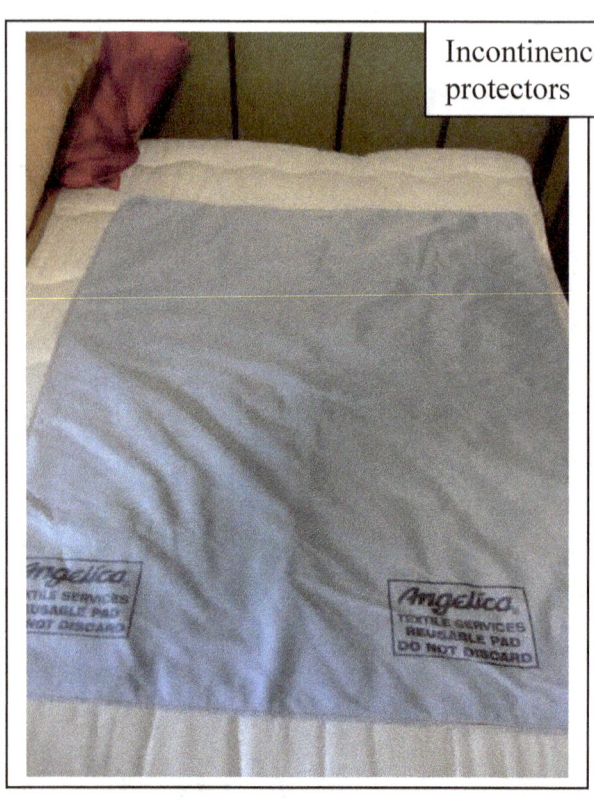

Incontinence mattress protectors

Picker-upper

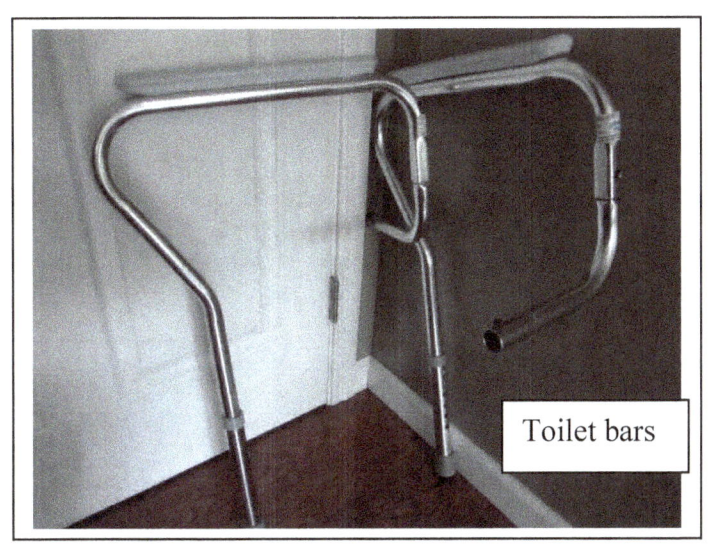
Toilet bars

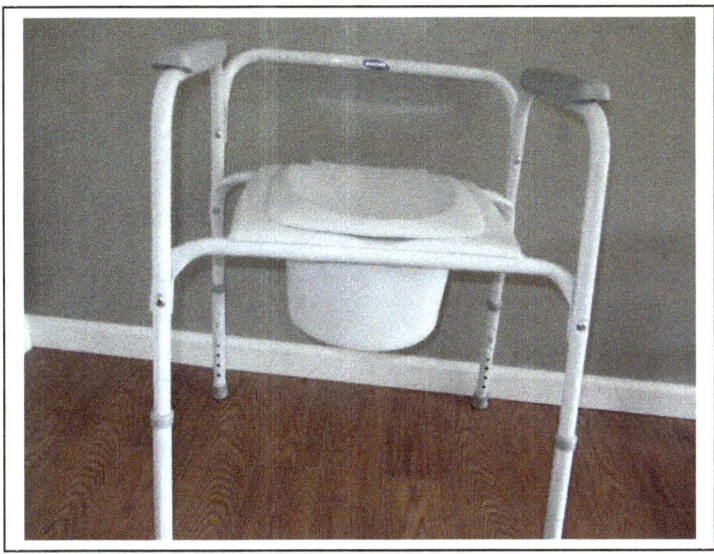
Portable bed-side commode

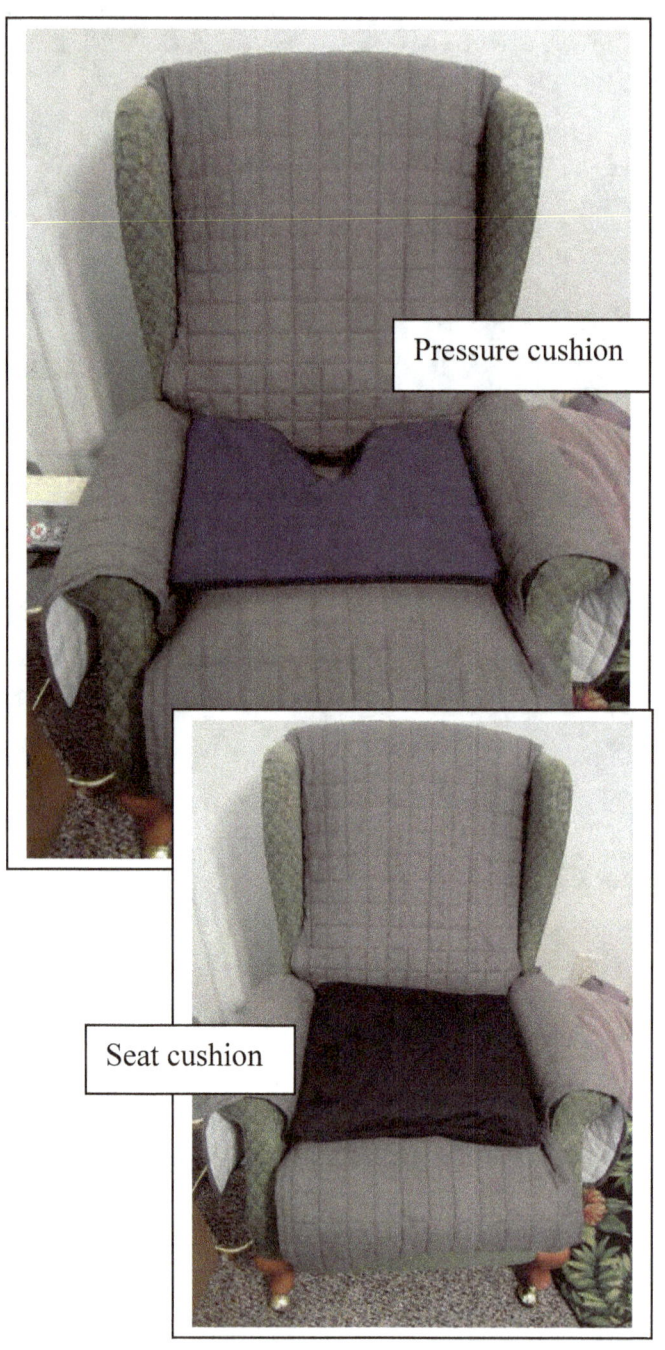

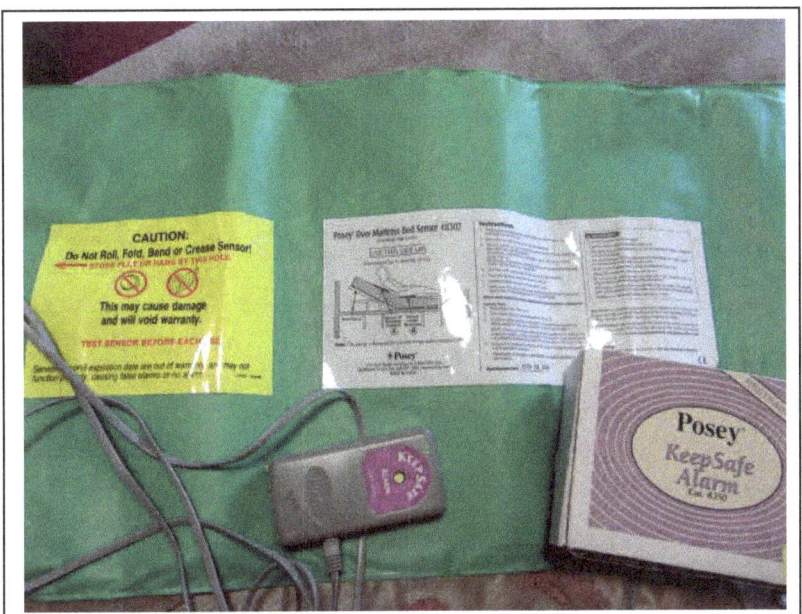

Posey Bed Alarm

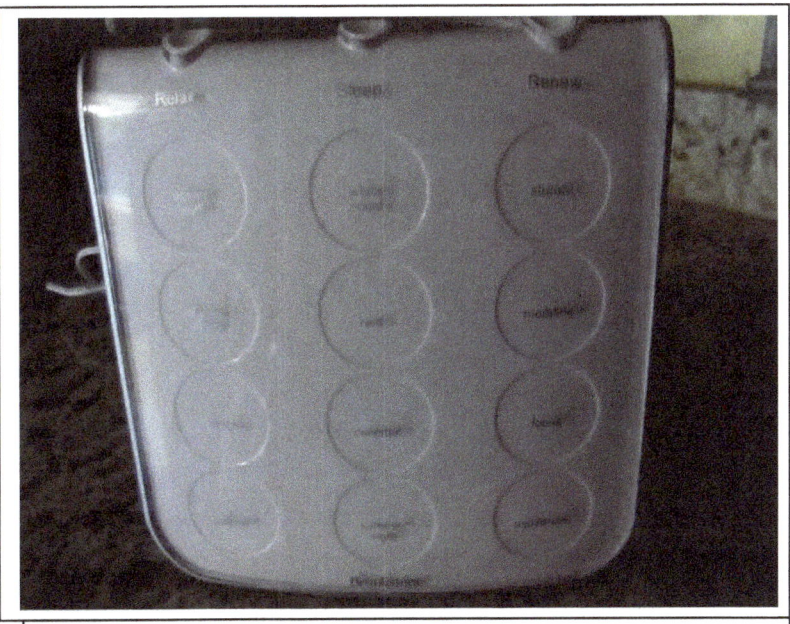

Sound machine - soothing rain forest, birds, ocean waves, white noise, etc.

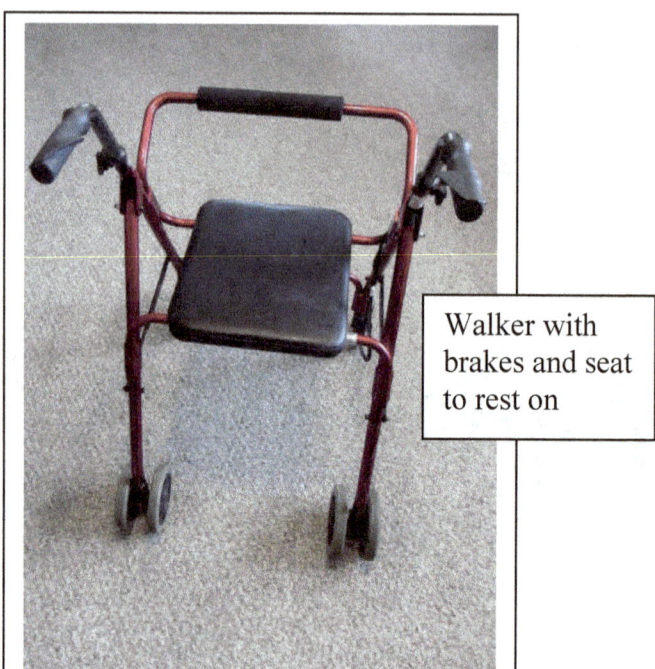

Walker with brakes and seat to rest on

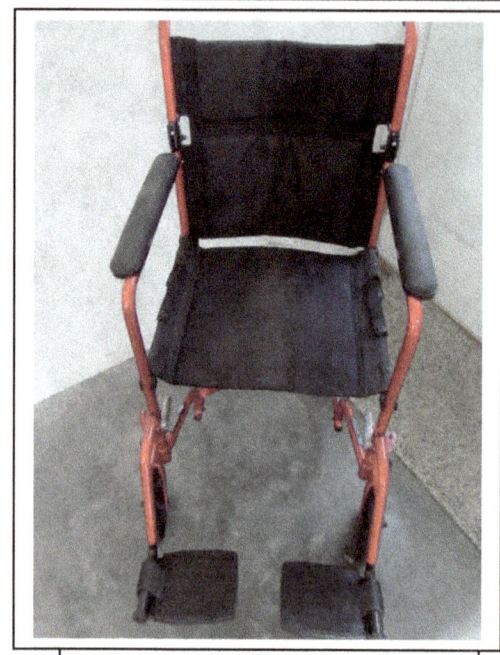

Wheel chair with fold up feet

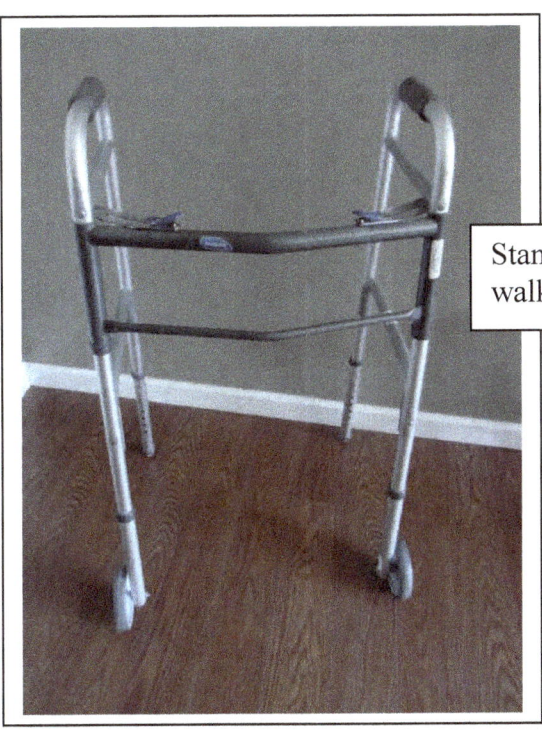

Stand-alone walker

Gait Belt- stand behind the patient with your hand holding the belt to assist the patient standing and walking.

Hand held shower hose

Baby monitor

Dementia Comment and Translation

Comment	Translation
My back is broke	My back hurts.
I'm dying/I'm having a heart attack	I'm scared about what's happening to me. I'm having a panic attack.
I'm starving	I've lost the sense of being full. I can't remember what or when I last ate.
I'm full	I've lost the sense of being hungry. I don't think I need to eat.
I want to go home	I'm scared and confused and want to feel safe and secure. I'm ready to die and be with God.
I can't hear	I hear you speaking but I no longer understand the words you are saying.
I can't see	I see letters but I can't piece them together into words. I no longer understand what words mean.
I don't like it here	I don't like what's happening to me. I don't want to be alive in this world in my declined physical and mental condition anymore.
Don't throw me away	Don't leave me. Don't put me in a nursing home apart from you.
The nice lady that takes care of me	My wife
Boy	My son
I'm reading	I'm turning the pages in the book.

Glossary

Alzheimer's – Disease which accounts for 60-80% of dementia cases. The following are the 10 most common symptoms: memory loss that disrupts daily life; challenges in planning or solving problems; difficulty completing familiar tasks at home, at work or at leisure; confusion with time or place; trouble understanding visual images and spatial relationships; new problems with words in speaking or writing; misplacing things and losing the ability to retrace steps; decreased or poor judgment; withdrawal from work or social activities; changes in mood and personality.

Aricept (Donepezil)– Prescription drug approved by the FDA in 1996 to help alleviate symptoms of all stages of dementia.

Atrial fibrillation - Arrhythmia - too fast, too slow, or irregular heartbeat causing poor blood flow.

Conservator – A protector appointed by a judge to manage the financial affairs and/or daily life of another due to physical or mental limitations, or old age.

Dementia – Dementia is a general term for a decline in mental ability severe enough to interfere with daily life. Dementia is not a specific disease. It describes a wide range of symptoms which are more than the normal part of aging.

- Stage 1 (mild dementia) – This stage can last from 2-4 years. In the early stages of Alzheimer's, a person may function independently. He or she may still drive, work and be part of social activities. Despite this, the person may feel as if he or she is having memory lapses, such as forgetting familiar words or the location of everyday objects. Friends, family or neighbors begin to notice difficulties. During a detailed medical interview, doctors may be able to detect problems in memory or concentration. Common difficulties include: problems describing the right word or name; trouble remembering names when introduced to new people; difficulty performing tasks in social or work settings; forgetting material just read; losing or misplacing a valuable object; increasing difficulty planning or organizing.

- <u>Stage 2 (moderate dementia)</u> - This stage may last from 2-10 years. These patients can no longer perform routine tasks, has lost their short term memory, lost the ability to know day and time, becomes lost or loses things, doesn't understand relationships, needs to be accompanied everywhere, becomes very suspicious and may have hallucinations. Moderate Alzheimer's is typically the longest stage. As the disease progresses, there will be word confusion, frustration, anger and unexpected behavior – such as refusal to bathe. Damage to nerve cells in the brain can make it difficult to express thoughts and perform routine tasks. At this point, symptoms will be noticeable to others. They include: forgetfulness of recent and past events, personal history, moodiness or withdrawal especially in socially or mentally challenging situations, inability to recall address or telephone number, high school or college experiences, confusion about immediate location, date or time of day. Expect that help will be needed to choose proper clothing for the season or occasion. Expect there may be trouble controlling bladder and bowels. Anticipate changes in sleep patterns (daytime sleeping, nighttime restlessness); increased risk of wandering and becoming lost. There will be personality and behavioral changes, including suspiciousness, delusions and compulsive repetitive actions, such as hand-wringing or tissue shredding.

- <u>Stage 3 (advanced dementia)</u> - This stage can last from 1-2 years. In the final stage of the disease, individuals lose the ability to respond to their environment, to carry on a conversation and, eventually, to control movement. They may still say words or phrases, but communicating pain becomes difficult. As memory and cognitive skills continue to worsen, personality changes may take place and individuals need extensive help with daily activities. At this stage, individuals require full-time, around-the-clock assistance with daily personal care. They lose awareness of recent experiences as well as surroundings. They experience changes in physical abilities, including the ability to walk, sit, and eventually, swallow. They have increasing difficulty communicating. They become vulnerable to infections, especially pneumonia.

<u>Depakote</u> – Prescription drug used to treat Post Traumatic Stress and bi-polar mania.

<u>DHR</u> – The Department of Human Resources. Helps protect children and vulnerable adults from abuse, neglect or exploitation. They also provide a variety of services to citizens with many programs designed for low-income families.

<u>Dupuytrens Contracture</u> – A hand deformity that usually develops over years. The condition affects a layer of tissue that lies under the skin of the palm. Knots of tissue form under the skin — eventually creating a thick cord that pull the fingers into a bent, claw-like position. The affected fingers can't be straightened, which complicates or prohibits everyday activities.

<u>Durable Power of Attorney</u> – A legal document that gives someone chosen the power to act in your place. In case you become mentally incapacitated, you'll need what are known as "durable" powers of attorney for medical care and finances.

Executor – A person or institution appointed by a testator (a person who has made a will or given a legacy) to carry out the terms of the will.

Failure to Thrive (FTT) - Failure to thrive in elderly persons is defined by The Institute of Medicine as weight loss of more than 5%, decreased appetite, poor nutrition, and physical inactivity, often associated with dehydration, depression, immune dysfunction, and low cholesterol. Failure to thrive is not a single disease or medical condition; rather, it's a non-specific manifestation of an underlying physical, mental, or psychosocial condition.

Galantamine – Prescription drug approved by the FDA in 2001 to treat mild to moderate Alzheimer's disease.

Guardian ad Litem – A person the court appoints to investigate what solutions would be in the "best interests" of a person. The Guardian ad Litem acts only for the duration of a legal action. Courts appoint these special representatives for infants, minors, and mentally incompetent persons, all of whom generally need help protecting their rights in court.

Hepatitis C – Infection of the liver. Symptoms include: jaundice (a condition that causes yellow eyes and skin, as well as dark urine); stomach pain; loss of appetite; nausea; fatigue. The virus spreads through the blood or body fluids of an infected person. Contagious by sharing drugs and needles; having sex, especially with an STD, an HIV infection, several partners, or rough sex; being stuck by infected needles; birth - a mother can pass it to a child. May lead to liver cancer or cirrhosis (scarring of the liver).

Hospice – A special concept of care designed to provide comfort and support to patients and their families when a life-limiting illness no longer responds to cure-oriented treatments. Hospice care neither prolongs life nor hastens death. Hospice care addresses the patient's physical, emotional, social and spiritual needs. Hospice care also helps the patient's family caregivers. It is usually ordered by the patient's doctor when a determination is made that the patient has six months or less to live.

Incapacitated – A person who is diagnosed as being mentally ill, senile, or suffering from some other debility that prevents them from managing their own affairs may be declared mentally incompetent by a court of law. When a person is judged to be incompetent, a guardian is appointed to handle the person's property and personal affairs. The legal procedure for declaring a person incompetent consists of three steps: (1) a motion for a competency hearing, (2) a psychiatric or psychological evaluation, and (3) a competency hearing. Probate courts usually handle competency proceedings, which guarantee the allegedly incompetent person Due Process of Law. If a person does not comprehend the nature and consequences of a contract when it is formed, they are regarded as having mental incapacity. A person who has been declared incompetent in a court proceeding lacks the legal capacity to enter into a contract with another. Such a person is unable to consent to a contract, since the court has determined that he does not understand the obligations and effects of a contract. A contract made by such a person is void and without any legal effect. If there has been no adjudication of mental incompetency, a contract made by a mentally incapacitated individual is Voidable by them. This means that the person can legally declare the contract void, making it unenforceable. However, a voidable contract can be ratified by the incompetent person if the person recovers the capacity to contract.

Lactulose – Prescription laxative for bowel impaction. A synthetic sugar used to treat constipation.

Lasix – A diuretic. Used to treat fluid retention (edema) in people with congestive heart failure, liver disease, or a kidney disorder such as nephrotic syndrome. This medication is also used to treat high blood pressure (hypertension).

Living Will – Also called a directive to physicians or advance directive, a document that lets people state their wishes for end-of-life medical care, in case they become unable to communicate their decisions. It has no power after death.

Mini-Mental Exam - The Mini-Mental Status Examination is a quick way to quantify cognitive function and screen for cognitive loss. It tests the individual's orientation, attention, calculation, recall, language and motor skills. Each section of the test involves a related series of questions or commands. The individual receives one point for each correct answer. The maximum number of points on the test is 30. If the patient scores below 20, they are considered to have cognitive impairment.

Mirtazapine (Remeron) – Prescription drug used to treat major depressive disorder.

Morton's Neuroma – A neuroma is a thickening of nerve tissue that may develop in various parts of the body. The most common neuroma in the foot is a Morton's neuroma, which occurs between the third and fourth toes. It is sometimes referred to as an intermetatarsal neuroma. "Intermetatarsal" describes its location in the ball of the foot between the metatarsal bones. Neuromas may also occur in other locations in the foot. The thickening, or enlargement of the nerve that defines a neuroma is the result of compression and irritation of the nerve. This compression creates enlargement of the nerve, eventually leading to permanent nerve damage and requires surgery.

Namenda – Prescription drug approved by the FDA in 2003 to treat symptoms of moderate to severe Alzheimer's disease – usually to aid in daily functioning.

Plantar Fasciitis – A major cause of heel pain. The plantar fascia is the flat band of tissue (ligament) that connects heel bone to toes. It supports the arch of the foot. If the plantar fascia is strained, it gets weak, swollen, and irritated (inflamed). The heel or bottom of the foot hurts when standing or walking. It can happen in one foot or both feet. Plantar fasciitis is caused by straining the ligament that supports the arch. Repeated strain can cause tears in the ligament.

PTS – Post Traumatic Stress. A condition of persistent mental and emotional stress occurring as a result of injury or severe psychological shock, typically involving disturbance of sleep and constant vivid recall of the experience, with dulled responses to others and to the outside world. Symptoms may include flashbacks, nightmares and severe anxiety, as well as uncontrollable thoughts about the event. Trauma survivors who have PTSD may have trouble with their close family relationships or friendships. Their symptoms can cause problems with trust, closeness, communication, and problem solving, which may affect the way the survivor acts with others. In turn, the way a loved one responds to him or her affects the trauma survivor.

Restraining Order - A temporary court order issued to prohibit an individual from carrying out a particular action, especially approaching or contacting a specified person. Used by a court to protect a person or entity, and the general public, in a situation involving alleged domestic violence, harassment, stalking, or sexual assault. Each restraining order has its own terms as to how far away a defendant must stay from the complaintant. Typically it is 50 or 100 feet. If you become aware that the other party is within that protection zone, it is up to you to remove yourself from the location.

SCALF – Specialty Care Assisted Living Facility. This usually means the facility has additional trained staff and special architectural features such as a "lock down" wing to assure the safety and health of residents with Alzheimer's disease or other forms of dementia.

Sundowning – A psychological phenomenon associated with increased confusion and restlessness in patients with dementia. Most commonly associated with Alzheimer's disease, but also found in those with mixed dementia. The term "sundowning" was coined due to the timing of the patient's confusion. For patients with sundowning syndrome, a multitude of behavioral problems begin to occur in the evening or while the sun is setting. Sundowning seems to occur more frequently during the middle stages of Alzheimer's disease and mixed dementia.

TIA - Transient Ischemic Attack, or mini-stroke caused by a clot. The only difference between a stroke and TIA is that with TIA the blockage is transient (temporary). TIA symptoms occur rapidly and last a relatively short time. Most TIAs last less than five minutes; the average is about a minute. When a TIA is over, it usually causes no permanent injury to the brain. However, about a third of people who experience TIA go on to have a stroke within a year.

Reference

1. Mace, Nancy, M.A. and Rabins, Peter, M.D., M.P.H. 1999. ***The 36-Hour Day***. New York: Wellness Central
2. Schenk, David. 2001. ***The Forgetting: Alzheimer's: Portrait of An Epedemic.*** New York: Doubleday
3. Lueckenotte, Deanna, BA, LBSW, CALM, LNFA. 2009. ***Alzheimer's: Days Gone By***. Indiana: Author House
4. Shagam, Janet. 2013. ***An Unintended Journey***. New York: Prometheus Books
5. Schaeffer, Juliann. 2016. ***Music Therapy in Dementia Treatment – Recollection Through Sound***. Pennsylvania: Great Valley Publishing Co., Inc.
6. Morris, Virginia. 2004. ***How to Care for Aging Parents***. New York: Workman Publishing
7. Amarnick, D.O., Claude. 2001. ***Don't Put Me in a Nursing Home.*** Florida: Garrett Publishing, Inc.
8. Tanzig, Rudolph and Parson, Ann. 2000. ***Decoding Darkness – The Search for the Genetic Causes of Alzheimer's Disease***. Massachusetts: Perseus Publishing
9. Levin, Nora Jean. 1990. ***How to Care for Your Parents.*** Washington: Storm King Press
10. Broyles, Frank. 2006. ***Coach Broyle's Playbook for Alzheimer's Caregivers***. Retrieved from http://www.alzheimersreadingroom.com/2008/04/playbook-for-alzheimer-caregivers.html
11. Alzheimer's Association. 2016. ***What We Know Today About Alzheimer's Disease and Dementia***. Retrieved from http://www.alz.org/research/science/alzheimers_research.asp
12. Alzheimer's Association. 2016. ***Major Milestones in Alzheimer's and Brain Research.*** Retrieved from https://alzreadinessproject.com/#discovery-timeline
13. Alzheimer's Association. 2015. ***Behaviors-How to Respond When Dementia Causes Unpredictable***

Behavior. Retrieved from http://www.alz.org/national/documents/brochure_behaviors.pdf
14. Alzheimer's Foundation of America. 2016. ***Education and Care Music.*** Retrieved from http://alzfdn.org/EducationandCare/musictherapy.html
15. UCI Irvine. 2015. ***What Causes Alzheimer's.*** Retrieved from https://www.mind.uci.edu/alzheimers-disease/what-is-alzheimers/what-causes-alzheimers/
16. AARP. Aug/Sept 2016. Caregiving Videos. Caregiving Stress. Caregiving Guilt. ***Caregiving:The Circle of Love; Caregiving Dahil Mahal Kita (Because I Love You); Stepping Up: Stories of Jazz and Caregiving.*** Retrieved from http://aarp.org/multiculturalcaregiving
17. AARP. Aug 2015 Bulletin. ***The Healing Power of Music.*** Retrieved from http://aarp.org/health/brain-health/info-2015/music-therapy-for-alzheimers.html
18. APD Cares. 2016. ***Common Signs of Abuse, Neglect, and Exploitation***. Retrieved from http://apd.myflorida.com/zero-tolerance/common-signs/

www.ingramcontent.com/pod-product-compliance
Lightning Source LLC
Chambersburg PA
CBHW071926290426
44110CB00013B/1490